Marriage

Questions Women Ask

Marriage

Questions
Women Ask

Gloria Gaither

Gigi Graham Tchividjian

Susan Alexander Yates

Christianity Today, Inc.

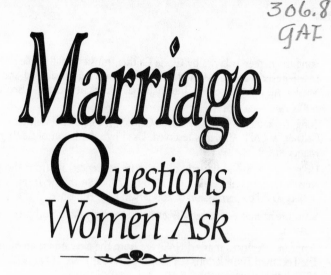

in conjunction with

MULTNOMAH
Portland, Oregon

Song in chapter 1: Lyrics by Gloria Gaither, music by Bill Smiley, "Things that Last Forever" (©1986 Gaither Music Co., Birdwing Music, Kid and the Squid Music). All rights reserved. International copyright secured. Used by permission.

Song in chapter 4: Lyrics by Gloria Gaither, music by Bill Gaither (© William J. Gaither, ASCAP). All rights reserved. Used by permission of Gaither Copyright Management.

Unless otherwise indicated, all Scripture references are from the Holy Bible: New International Version, © 1973, 1978, 1984 by the International Bible Society. Used by permission of Zondervan Bible Publishers.

Scripture references marked KJV are from the Holy Bible: Authorized King James Version.

Scripture references marked NASB are from the New American Standard Bible, The Lockman Foundation, © 1960, 1962, 1963, 1968, 1971, 1972, 1973, 1975, 1977. Used by permission.

Cover design by Bruce De Roos
MARRIAGE: QUESTIONS WOMEN ASK
© 1992 by Christianity Today, Inc.
Published by Multnomah Press
10209 SE Division Street
Portland, Oregon 97266

Multnomah Press is a ministry of
Multnomah School of the Bible
8435 NE Glisan Street
Portland, Oregon 97220

Printed in the United States of America.

Library of Congress Cataloging-in-Publication Data
Gaither, Gloria.
     Marriage—questions women ask / Gloria Gaither, Gigi Graham Tchividjian, Susan Alexander Yates.
          p.   cm. —(TCW)
     ISBN 0-88070-460-8
     1. Marriage. 2. Marriage—Religious aspects—Christianity. 3. Interpersonal relations. I. Tchividjian, Gigi. II. Yates, Susan Alexander. III. Title. IV. Series
HQ734.G14   1992
306.81—dc20   91-41259
                                                                              CIP

92 93 94 95 96 97 98 99 00 01 - 10 9 8 7 6 5 4 3 2 1

CONTENTS

SECTION THREE
Marriage Spirituality

MAKING GOOD MARRIAGES BETTER

arly in the development of this book, Gigi Graham Tchividjian, the mother of seven and married for twenty-eight years to Stephan, a psychologist, shared the following story about her grandparents Nelson and Virginia Bell:

My grandparents had as close to an ideal marriage as I have ever seen. My grandfather made it a point to express his appreciation for his wife—in word and in deed. For instance, I rarely saw him go into the living room, put his feet up, and watch the news while Grandmother was in the kitchen cleaning up. Rather, he would help her with the dishes. His rationale: it afforded him yet another opportunity to be with his wife.

My grandmother expressed pride in her husband and his work as a surgeon. She, too, wanted to be with him whenever possible. She would never go to sleep until he was home from being on call (in those days, doctors still made "house calls"). And as much as possible, she would go with him whenever he made his hospital visits or attended business luncheons, preferring to sit in the car and work on crossword puzzles by the light of the glove compartment than stay home by herself. She often took one of us grandchildren along to keep her company.

As they got older, my grandfather had to care for Grandmother. My mother came into their house one day and found Grandfather—who was not a well man himself—on his hands and knees putting Grandma's stockings on her feet. He looked up with a big smile and said, "You know, the greatest privilege of my life is taking care of your mother."

My grandfather had been a pioneer missionary, an author and a surgeon, was founder of Christianity Today *magazine, and served on the boards of numerous religious organizations, but his greatest privilege was to be on his knees putting on his wife's stockings.*

We share this story with you because we feel it expresses the kind of marriage that God intends for each one of us. A marriage earmarked by mutual commitment and respect, and expressed in the selfless loving of a servant's heart. Such marriage is, to paraphrase Scripture, an opportunity to lose one's self in another's life—only to find yourself and experience the joy and fulfillment God intends wives and husbands to have in this, one of his choicest gifts.

How to move in the direction of this kind of marriage is the purpose of this book. *Questions Women Ask About Marriage* is for the woman who is not content with "just" a good marriage, but who wants her marriage to truly become everything God wants it to be.

To that end, each chapter is based on a question that women are likely to ask sometime in their married life. Each question represents an issue or concern that has generated high interest and attention from the readers of *Today's Christian Woman* magazine over the past five years.

Supplementing the discussion of these "universal" concerns are excerpts from the pages of *Today's Christian Woman* magazine, and a section entitled "Make It Happen," offering practical ways you can quickly and easily implement the specific suggestions made in each chapter.

About the Contributors

Answering the fourteen questions posed in this book are three women whose own marriages have grown despite the usual slings and arrows of too many commitments and too little time.

— ◦◦◦◦ —

Gloria Gaither and her husband, Bill, have been partners in marriage and ministry for twenty-eight years. Together they've written hundreds of songs, recorded fifty-four albums, and performed countless concerts. But one of their greatest accomplishments has been establishing a home that attracts people. As Gloria said, "The table always had an extra place setting" for one of the kids' friends. They have three children, the youngest now in college.

Bill and Gloria met while teaching at the same high school. Gloria was substituting for a French teacher and Bill taught English.

"We started going to lunch and talking about politics and literature. We even directed some plays together. And by that summer, we were engaged.

"We loved teaching and literature. And then we started writing these songs . . ." and from there they went on to shape the course of contemporary Christian music.

Bill and Gloria have a mutually nourishing relationship. They welcome each other's input; they thrive on sharing new discoveries; they feed the other's creativity. And they argue.

"I wouldn't give you two cents for an 'idyllic' marriage," Gloria said. "I'd be bored out of my skull. I like interaction." And her expressiveness comes out clearly in this book.

— ◦◦◦◦ —

Another woman we invited to contribute is *Gigi Graham Tchividjian*. The circumstances of her engagement and marriage were the most unusual of the group.

"My father-in-law came to know the Lord by reading one of my father's books," Gigi said. (She is the eldest child of Billy and Ruth Graham.) "My father-in-law is Armenian by background and was living in Switzerland. He was so changed by his new faith that he decided to bring my father to Switzerland to hold a crusade. My father-in-law invited the whole family over for the summer."

There Gigi met Stephan, who was twenty-one at the time. Since she was only fourteen, Gigi didn't think much about him.

A few years later, when she was in her first year of college, Gigi's mother mentioned receiving a nice letter from Stephan. What she didn't say was that the letter contained a proposal of marriage. Stephan felt directed by the Lord to propose to Gigi and, if her parents concurred, they were to pass the letter on to Gigi.

"I read his letter," Gigi recalled, "and a particular phrase really struck me. He said that if it was the Spirit of God who had told him, then he believed the Spirit would tell me." She continued to pray and read Scripture, and everything began to point to Stephan being God's choice for her.

Four days before Christmas, Gigi's father called and invited Stephan to spend Christmas with the family. "I went to the airport to pick him up," Gigi said, "and as soon as I saw him I knew I was to say yes. I had no emotion; I didn't feel love; I just knew. After I said yes to Stephan, the Lord began to give me love for him."

After ten years of working in the family business and living in Europe and the Middle East, Stephan decided to make a career change. They moved to the States so he could pursue a degree in psychology and set up a practice in counseling.

The family now lives in Florida, where Stephan has an active practice. Many of his clients are working through marital difficulties, so he proved a valuable resource for Gigi as she addressed the questions in this book. Gigi is author of several books, her latest is *Weather of the Heart* (Multnomah Press, 1990).

— ❦ —

Completing our circle of friends is *Susan Alexander Yates*. Author of the book *And Then I Had Kids—Encouragement for Mothers of Young Children* (Wolgemuth & Hyatt), Susan is also a model, an actress, and a popular retreat speaker. But all that is secondary to being a wife and mother. She and her husband, John, are the parents of five children. John pastors The Falls Church (Episcopal) in Falls Church, Virginia.

"We were simply best friends who decided to get married," Susan says.

Their five children came within seven years—a girl, two boys, and then twin girls. Susan said, "Before the twins were born, I felt that I was coping pretty well with the demands of marriage, three children, and a busy church. I had a sense of pride about how I was doing with my family and with the Lord. And then the twins arrived, blowing apart my smugness and replacing it with an overwhelming sense of failure. But it was the failure that God used in my life to humble me and to gently show me that I needed to rely on him in a deeper way."

Married twenty-two years, with busy schedules, John and Susan have learned to build in "traditions" to insure that their own relationship doesn't get overlooked in the midst of many demands. One such tradition is taking the first fifteen minutes when John gets home from work simply to talk with each other, to share about their day, and to touch base before the evening's activities get underway. Susan offers many such practical ideas for strengthening the marriage relationship throughout the book.

— ᕙᐷᕷ —

Together, Gloria, Gigi, and Susan interacted with us in a two-day forum in Chicago in September 1990, and later were individually interviewed by phone and in person over the following twelve months. From their comments were constructed the chapters making up this book.

These women speak openly and honestly from their own experience, and from hours spent helping friends and acquaintances face hard times in their marriages. And they naturally refer time and again to the Bible, as it provides the basis for their relationships.

What you read in this book is immensely practical and completely scriptural. And it is our hope that you will be able to pick up several "great truths" that will enable you to make your marriage a rich, fulfilling relationship.

Louise A. Ferrebee and Rebecca K. Grosenbach, editors

THE EXPECTATIONS TRAP

nyone who's married knows the operations of Marriage, Inc., are a twenty-four hour balancing act. There's finding quality *and* quantity time with your husband. Finding time with your children. Finding time with your parents. And, somewhere, usually near the bottom of the list, there's finding time for yourself.

Is it any wonder we never have enough time!

And if life isn't complicated enough, we have the media daily feeding us a steady diet of the ways and means to a perfect marriage (complete with perfect bodies and perfect sex), perfect children, and perfect fulfillment—inside *and* outside the home. While common sense dictates that such perfection is more Fantasyland than Main Street America, such myths have tragically become a part of our collective psyche. They have become a primary—perhaps *the* primary—motivation behind our endless longing and striving for a reality that can never be reached.

Is it any wonder so many women have grown tired and dissatisfied with their lives and relationships? Is it any wonder so many of us have put up our hands in frustration and asked, "Is that all there is?"

In the following chapters, Gloria, Gigi, and Susan talk about the debilitating role false expectations play in the makeup of our marriage and family life, specifically in our relationship to husband and children, our relationship to parents and in-laws, and our individual desire for personal growth and development. They also share with us what kind of expectations can be *realistically* set up in each of these areas—expectations that can eventually lead away from on-going relational frustrations and lead to personal and marital fulfillment.

Chapter 1

AM I EXPECTING TOO MUCH FROM MARRIAGE?
Gloria Gaither

nrealistic expectations plague American marriages. Dreams of endless passion and encouraging words fill newlywed hearts and minds—only to fall victim to the first fight, or the first "Not tonight, dear. I'm too tired."

And Christian men and women aren't immune. Indeed, the church has manufactured its own unique brand of false expectations: a euphoric picture of marriage where bunches of pleasantries fill each day and nary a cross word is spoken. After all, Christians are supposed to be happy and content. Always.

Little wonder then that when "euphoria" butts up against reality, husbands and wives don't know what to think.

What, then, should our expectations be—and how should we keep them realistic?

The place to begin is not in the media, not in "churchianity," but the Bible, God's holy word. As incredibly "simple" as that may sound, it's advice more of us need to take to heart. Without a head and heart knowledge of the Scriptures, we'll be unable to discern the lies and hurts of a thousand false messages.

I had this driven home to me years ago when my now twenty-six-year-old daughter was fourteen.

For about two years, Suzanne had made it a point to read her Bible every night before she went to bed. One day, as I was tucking her into bed, she asked if I would like to hear the particular passage she was reading that night, and I said, "Sure."

When she finished, she asked: "Mother, do you know why I read like this every night?" "No," I said.

"Well," she replied, "you don't know what it's like at school. Sometimes I have nightmares that you come to school and walk down the hall and see and hear what I see and hear. But," she continued, "what really scares me is that by the end of the day, I begin to think what I see and hear is normal. It doesn't bother me anymore.

"So," she concluded, "when I come home at night and pick up the Bible, it really doesn't matter what I read. Reading God's Word helps me to know what God thinks about things."

Out of the mouths of children. Suzanne's profound observation is exactly the reason why we need to be in the Word. Not to prove a theological point. Not to fulfill a duty. But to better understand the character and intent of God, so that he can set the tone for the choices, decisions, and operations of our lives.

Only then can we be in a position to take on the mixed messages of our culture.

———— ✤ ————

So then, what insights does the Bible give us about what to expect from marriage? Well, perhaps the loudest and clearest relational expectation set forth in Scripture is the reality of differing personalities and the subsequent interpersonal conflicts they tend to ignite.

Take the disciples. Jesus chose this motley crew on purpose, with an assortment of quirks and characteristics that are probably inherent in most marriages. One disciple was bombastic and never ran anything through his head before running it out of his mouth. Another disciple only ran things through his head and never out of his mouth. One disciple was a penny-pincher. And still another one was emotional and always embracing. Incredible!

In reading the gospel accounts, we get a pretty good sense of how these differing passions and personalities not only co-existed—but coexisted for the good of the Kingdom. We also see it was never easy.

Here, then, is a great lesson for any wife or husband: God can use our individual peculiarities and weaknesses—the very ones we bring into marriage—to build his Kingdom. And it is of this profoundly humbling truth that I need to remind myself whenever I'm bitter. Whenever I'm disappointed. Whenever I'm disillusioned that this man I married—who's supposed to be "perfect"—isn't.

Finding a Good Picture

One thing that helps me develop realistic expectations in marriage is to find role models. Develop friends of different ages you can go to and ask, "What were the early years like for you? How do you work through conflict?" A great deal can be learned from role models.

—Susan

In my despair I can either give up, become a cynic, or I can be driven to my knees.

Ideally, of course, we should be driven to our knees. But that action won't come unless I'm committed to something bigger than my marriage. After all, while I'm in love with Bill, there are times he's downright unlovely. And there are days I'm far less than he thought I'd be. On those particular days some wonderful philosophical belief in the institution of marriage doesn't make us stay in one.

The only way a marriage can survive the inevitable tough times is a commitment to something bigger than the marriage itself. And the only thing bigger than my commitment to Bill is my commitment to God.

Bill and I are two very energetic people. We both have ego needs. What has saved us time and again when those egos collide is our desire to live with an eternal perspective—to have the mind and heart of Christ in everything we do. Without God, it would be very easy to leave a marriage when an impasse is reached, or when something isn't done "my way." But with God, we are commanded to put Kingdom achievements before personal achievements.

Ultimately, commitment to Christ gives perspective to any and everything encountered in marriage. When money is tight, or some business deal is not going the way we'd planned, Bill will often say, "You know what would put this in perspective? If the phone rang and we were told one of our children had cancer."

One day Bill and I actually made a list of what really counts—a list of "things that last forever." I recommend this exercise to you. I guarantee, your list will be pretty short: your relationships, your integrity, your commitments—these are the things that last forever. When we finished our list, we said that if it isn't on the list, then it's not big enough to disrupt our family.

If two people can agree on that list, it can bring a breath of freedom into a marriage. Your personal goals and aspirations are no longer "life and death" issues. Rather, they are "take it or leave it" issues in the light of these of more eternal concern.

Our list became a song. Our daughter Suzanne had Bill sing it at her wedding.

Don't Work so Hard

I've been examining the relationship between Abraham and Sarah and other Old Testament couples. The biblical picture is that marriage was for companionship and procreation. They seemed to have very simple expectations, like mutual respect and support.

But in our society married couples are supposed to be each other's best friends. We're supposed to be the greatest lovers, we're supposed to be attractive physically, and the list goes on. And I wonder if our Americanized, even Christian, idea of marriage is really unattainable.

—Gigi

"Things That Last Forever"

> I can't think of many places
> I'd leave it all to go—
> Can't think of many things
> I'd die to hold.
> The list of what is priceless
> Is very short, indeed—
> And there are not very many things

I find I really need.
So here's my simple creed:

> *The things that last forever,*
> > *The things that never die—*
> > *I'll give myself each day I live*
> > *For what will never, never die—*
> > *I will give myself away*
> > *For things that will never die.*

To know a love that's lasting
Forgiveness without blame
A peace that through the pressure still remains
The simple joys of living
My family and my friends,
Relationships that go on after
Space and time shall end
Thank you, Lord, for them.

To rescue someone dying,
To lift a fallen child,
To hurt when someone's hurting
To walk the second mile.

> *The things that last forever,*
> > *The things that never die—*
> > *I'll give myself each day I live*
> > *For what will never, never die—*
> > *I will give myself away*
> > *For things that will never die.*

Only a transformation of our fallen nature can enable us to become one in our diversity—perhaps the ultimate expectation in marriage. It is not in our consensus that we are at one, but in our commitment to something bigger than any of us.

Into the marriage crucible we offer many differing opinions and attitudes, personalities and passions. But out of that crucible comes the promise of new ideas and larger truths, to be mutually shared for the benefit and growth of husband and wife.

Thus Christian marriage is not to be seen as an "I win, you lose" or an "I lose, you win" proposition. Rather, God's expectation of marriage is that it become a "He wins" situation, where man and woman commit to each other, becoming all God wants them to be.

Only God Can Alter a Personality
Gloria Gaither

Unrealistic expectations aren't always the reason for a disappointing marriage. Maybe you have a very realistic perception of what marriage should be, but your husband isn't the kind of mate he should be. Then the question becomes, "Should I try to change my husband if he doesn't meet my expectations?"

This question requires one of those "yes and no" responses. There are some ways we can help our spouses become what God intended them to be—and other things we simply have to accept. We really do need each other in order to develop godly character, but only God can alter personalities.

Even if we see character flaws, we should accept our husbands the way they are. This kind of acceptance is Christlike love without reservation. It is dangerous to allow yourself to think *I'd love him more if he were different.* Real love isn't conditional.

The truth is, we can't *make* our husbands into anything. But we can change ourselves. Ask, "What can I do to create an atmosphere in which my husband *can* change if he chooses to?" or "Is there something I can do to make it easier for him to change?" "Will he be more inspired to change if I display the kind of character I desire to see in him?" "Will he be more likely to change if I stop nagging? Show an interest in football? Learn to be more knowledgeable about political and international affairs?"

Be the best mate you can be and your husband will find it easier to become his best self.

Turning Disappointment into Adventure
Marsha Crockett

We all expect something out of everything in life—from our toilet bowl cleaner to our marriage. In either case, when our expectations go unmet, we become disappointed. But unfulfilled marriage expectations are not as easily remedied as switching to another brand of cleanser.

The following game plan helped turn our marriage disappointments into an adventure in getting to know each other better. It may work for you, too.

The Object

To avoid feelings of disappointment
To develop a deeper understanding of each other
To define duties and responsibilities
To open the door for future communication
To correct mistaken assumptions

The Strategy

1. *Acknowledge expectations.* This is most difficult for newlyweds dealing with the "I-love-you-just-the-way-you-are" syndrome. Go ahead and let your husband know that you didn't expect him to work late every night.

2. *Put expectations in writing.* Before your husband and you jump into your discussion, individually take time to answer these questions: What is my spouse's role in our marriage? Specifically, how can my spouse fulfill that role? Then write down your conclusions.

3. *Communicate expectations.* Use as many forms of communication as possible. Be especially sensitive to unspoken words. Use touch to reassure and affirm one another. Now get comfy and share your ideas, giving your spouse a copy of your written expectations.

4. *Be willing to compromise.* Some expectations simply may be unreasonable. Just because your mom served meat and potatoes every night doesn't necessarily make it right for your lifestyle. If your spouse has expectations you can't meet, be honest and let him know why.

5. *Accept suggestions and a helping hand.* If your husband has an idea about how the house should be kept, be willing to try his method of achieving that goal. (My husband's method has worked like a charm for me.)

6. *Re-evaluate.* As long as there are people on this earth, there will be change. Be aware of it and realize your expectations should be molded by life's realities.

The Ground Rules

1. *This is not a battleground.* Both partners must agree to start with a consuming desire to fulfill one another's needs. If you notice your volume rising, be aware of this sensitive topic and come back to it later.

2. *Don't expect to change the unchangeable.* You're playing dirty if you tell your spouse, "Gee, I wish you were taller and blond." Or, "I expected your mother to treat me differently." You can't change physical traits or control your mother-in-law's actions or attitudes.

3. *Laugh a lot.* Although discussing expectations

can be serious business, try to have fun with it. When my husband told me he expected the windows to be washed every week, there was nothing else to do but laugh. He eventually saw the humor in it, and we settled on a once-a-month washing.

Winning

While this is a fun exercise, winning in marriage happens only when Christ crowns the head of the house. When we place our greatest life expectations in him, he never lets us down.

From Today's Christian Woman
(*May/June 1989*)

Make It Happen

1. Write down all the things you expect of your marriage relationship. Try to determine why you expect those things of your husband. Recognizing the source of your expectations might help eliminate some that are invalid.

2. As you review your list of expectations, ask yourself how you would feel if your husband said he expected the same things of you. Would you think he was being unrealistic? This won't fit in every case (he wouldn't expect you to be the major bread-winner if you weren't working outside the home) but it will help you evaluate some of the more emotional expectations such as being his primary source of motivation.

3. Create a mental picture of the man you believe your husband could be. Begin treating him as if he were that man, acting

on Goethe's words, "If you treat him as if he were what he ought
to be and could be, he will become that bigger and better man."

4. If you are aware of specific problems in your marriage
that are keeping it from being what it should be, pray for the
right words to tell your husband what concerns you. Don't let
the week pass before talking to him. The time to address a problem is *now*.

Chapter 2

IS THERE MORE TO INTIMACY THAN SEX?
Gloria Gaither

f God made any mistake (and he didn't!), it's that he put the most important decision in life right at the time when our hormones are raging. Little wonder, then, that we make a habit of confusing love with the urge to mate. And it's a confusion multiplied a thousandfold by everything in our culture—movies, books, magazines, and advertisements all paint the picture of love as unbridled hormonal passions. Nothing more, and, heaven forbid, nothing less.

Problems arise, however, when those hot emotions cool—even momentarily. And the truth of the matter is, they will. That's why, as important as our sexuality is, as important as the physical bond of marriage is, we've got to understand love as something more than "feelings." We've got to build a love for our husbands that will withstand the roller-coaster emotions of child-rearing, rat-race schedules, and the thousand-and-one demands that characterize each of our lives.

— ✦ —

The key to this bedrock love is understanding what true marital intimacy is all about. When Genesis 2:24 talks about

27

oneness, it's not *just* referring to the physical intimacy of husband and wife. It is also describing the spiritual, emotional, and psychological intimacy of two people who undress before each other and enter each other's body in the closest kind of union possible—soul to soul.

What this means in every day language is that physical intimacy, with all its pleasures and joys, is, in reality, only one aspect of marital love—not the be-all and end-all as our culture would have it. It is, instead, an outward expression of that soul-deep intimacy unfolding within the context of Christian marriage.

Sexual intercourse is like the consummation of a real estate deal. At closing, all you do is sign on the dotted line. But behind that simple signature are hours of negotiations, bank meetings, loan agreements, and discussions. Behind the marital "act" should be a husband and wife who take the time to talk to one another to understand the inner concerns, desires, dreams, passions, joys, and hurts of the other.

To actively counter today's tendency of going along signing lots of signatures—and making few, if any, investments—we have got to consciously take whatever steps are necessary to get inside the man we're married to—to know him; to understand him soul to soul.

—◆—

Such understanding takes time, of course. And that's difficult, especially for people like Bill and me who are in public ministry. When there is conflict, when there are things that ought to be discussed, things that ought to be hassled out, things that ought to be resolved, when do we deal with conflict? Do we do it before a concert? Do we do it on the bus with twenty other people present? Do we do it after a concert? Do we do it on Monday morning when Bill has a big business meeting and I'm off doing ten things I have to do? Do we do it on the one night we've saved all week to have dinner together—alone?

When?

For the Gaithers, key to building soul-deep intimacy has

been spontaneity, and a willingness to bring God in on the process at every juncture through prayer. Bill and I often find it necessary to seek God's wisdom, whether over a business matter, a situation with one of the kids, or something in our own marriage. In this way we not only communicate our reliance upon God (and admit our own weaknesses without him), but we communicate to each other the importance with which we hold these situations—and our commitment to make them stronger.

I do not have the wisdom to deal with the kind of complexities that are in our lives. And yet wonderful insights come to Bill

He's Always Changing

Rather than complain about the fact that our husbands are "not the men we married," we should be grateful for their change. In fact, we should allow them room to grow. After all, marriage would get boring pretty fast if we thought we knew everything about the person we lived with.

—Susan

and me when we dump something in God's lap and say "We're too dumb to deal with it. Give us a clue." And he does—not like a bolt from the blue, but as a gentle insight.

Mark That Date

Supplementing prayer and Gaither spontaneity have been scheduled together times. Believe it or not, I include our concerts here, because even with a thousand onlookers, I've found that public ministry with Bill provides unique glimpses into his personality and passions that, in turn, build a deeper intimacy between us. Perhaps there's a word here for any couple actively involved in Kingdom work, whether it be through a local church, a community ministry, whatever. Ministering together is a means for getting to know the other; for uncovering something deep within our partner; for growing together spiritually.

I remember one concert where Bill and I experienced mutual spiritual growth. It was out East; one of those really rowdy concerts. The people were very expressive. And they were plugged in to everything. They laughed when they were supposed to laugh. They cried when things were moving. They sang along. They clapped. The Holy Spirit was present.

At the end of the concert, the audience just kept clapping and clapping and clapping. It was great—for a while. But soon Bill and I began to sense that the crowd's appreciation was directed more toward us than to God. We could feel it. And it made us uncomfortable. Bill started a hymn to redirect the praise.

When we finally left the auditorium, we told each other that we would not let that happen again. Those people were mistaking the work of the Holy Spirit for the work of Bill and Gloria Gaither. So we wrote a song borne out of our concern that has since become quite well-known. And its first verse relates directly to that concert experience:

> *We'd like to thank you for your kindness,*
>> *Thank you for your love.*
>> *We've been in heavenly places,*
> *Felt blessings from above.*
>> *We've been sharing all the good things,*
>> *The family can afford.*
>> *But let's turn our praise t'ward heaven*
>> *And praise the Lord.*
>> *Let's just praise the Lord.*

That's one example where spiritual growth took place simultaneously because we both happened to minister together. Insights like that have come because of the spontaneity of the Holy Spirit in a specific situation; and because we minister together, that spiritual spontaneity has affected our marriage, enriched our marriage.

—⁓⬥⁓—

Time away from the concert stage has also enriched our marriage and helped build intimacy. And we have tried to consciously reserve family times when Bill and I can touch base.

Bill has been wonderful at protecting us from the craziness of the multiple demands on our lives. Early on he decided it was not God's will for us to say yes to every request made on our time. As Bill puts it, "He who hath no plan becomes the victim of everyone else's plan."

I remember one time the phone rang and it was someone on President Ford's staff. He wanted us to fly to Grand Rapids, Michigan, and sing for the President.

"I'm sorry," said Bill. "We're booked that night. It's our night to be home."

"That's great," said the fellow at the other end of the line. "If you're home, you'll be able to do it."

"No we can't," said Bill. He went on to explain that Monday is our night at home and that if we made exceptions for one person, our lives would soon be filled with exceptions.

So we didn't go. We didn't think one Monday night would make or break our kids or our marriage. But lots of other calls like that could.

There's a simple moral here: know where to draw the line.

A Lifetime Perspective

Intimacy—real intimacy—doesn't happen overnight. Knowing someone soul to soul takes a lifetime—and then some!

Case in point: where Bill and I are in our marriage just now. With our two daughters married and our son finishing college, we are both at change points. With each other's blessing we're both pursuing projects individually that we've been putting off because of more pressing—more important—commitments.

The challenge, the change point, is that for the first time, I am experiencing something exciting and important without Bill. The question then becomes, how *do* I include him? How do I share my excitement over my graduate research project on an American author with Bill, while not overwhelming him or, worse yet, boring him?

Uncovering ourselves to each other is tricky business. But without such revelation, our relationship will be empty. Like working out our salvation with fear and trembling, husbands and wives are called upon to know—and be known by—the other.

Where's the Romance?
Karen Dockrey

"I don't know how I ever lived without you. You make sense out of this crazy life of mine. I'm so glad God brought you into my life."

How we yearn for words like these from our husbands. Instead we hear, "What's for supper?" But don't give up. Keep in mind the following perspectives on "true romance."

Our perception of romance may be more a creation of Hollywood, not God. God described marriage with such concepts as unity and commitment. Notice these in the way your husband relates to you: talking about the simple things, working through decisions together, laughing to ease tension, helping you through both good and bad, easy and hard experiences.

Avoid the trap of clone romance. Too often we think romance must include certain words or actions. But "Let's take a walk" can be just as romantic as "How about a quiet candlelight dinner for two?" A phone call from your husband asking how to spell a word can convey just as much admiration as a dozen roses. Notice the ways your husband already expresses affection, such as teasing and tickling, or using humor to get you to think things through. Refuse to box him in by insisting on "prescribed" forms of romantic expression.

Discover sources of marital pleasure deeper than romance. Possibilities include clear communication, depending on each other for daily needs (one of you cooks supper while the other mows the lawn), savoring being together even when working on separate projects.

Imagine what life would be like without your husband. Too often day-to-day routines make us focus on the frustrations instead of the pleasures of marriage. Recall what first attracted you to your husband, then rediscover or rekindle those characteristics with a little appreciation.

Recognize the fascination in routine. Think about the interesting things you talk about over supper, or the funny stories you share at bedtime. Notice the pleasure of stacking the wood together, then complaining about sore muscles. Imagine life without shared meals, responsibilities, or celebrations.

Compliment your husband once each day. As you look for things to compliment, you'll discover all kinds of reasons to become re-romantically interested in the man you once couldn't wait to say "I do" to.

From Today's Christian Woman
(May/June 1989)

Make It Happen

1. Write down three things that first attracted you to your husband. Then add three additional things that you have come to appreciate during your marriage. Offer a prayer of thanksgiving for these qualities—then share them with your husband.

2. Make a list of the ways you think you've changed since being married. On another piece of paper, have your husband list the ways he thinks he's changed. Taking turns, try to guess what's on the other's list. Are any changes missing?

3. List one personal, professional (if you work outside the home), and spiritual need you would like your husband's help with. Share these with him at an appropriate time. And, if he's willing, have him do the same with you.

Chapter 3

HOW CAN I MAKE
THE MOST OF MY IN-LAW
RELATIONSHIPS?
Gigi Graham Tchividjian

have a young friend who recently married. Even before her wedding, she decided her mother-in-law was trying to control her and her husband's future. Without even giving the relationship time to develop, she felt compelled to put her foot down immediately about how involved her in-laws should be in her marriage.

My friend was bringing into her new relationship a bundle of preconceived notions of what in-law relationships would be like. She had probably heard her share of "horror" stories about in-laws and, rather than assume the best, prepared herself for the worse.

Looking back, I'm thankful I came to our marriage with a relatively open mind. After all, I was only seventeen when we married, and I had seen examples of loving, healthy in-law relationships in my family.

Stephan's parents had been divorced before we married, but his mother became one of my best friends. Here I was, trying to raise babies, adapt to a European culture—and making many mistakes—and she just kept encouraging me. Often, she would thank me for being such a wonderful wife to her only son. This built a precious relationship between my mother-in-law and myself.

Yet, I know in-law relations are not all sweetness and light. Stephan's father is very domineering and controlling and, needless to say, that imposed on my relationship to him—and to Stephan. We were the first children married out of both families, so it was hard for everyone to adjust. The situation was full of conflict until Stephan and I began to realize the importance of establishing our own family identity.

But despite all the potential for discordance as you bring two families together, in-laws can be a source of encouragement and wisdom that can not only strengthen you individually but strengthen your family as well. Although the relationship with my father-in-law has been difficult at times, I have also learned much from him.

Conflict Resolution: Have Patience

My own experiences have shown me that the key to resolving in-law problems is found in the book of Genesis where we're told to "leave and cleave." "For this reason a man will leave his father and mother and be united to his wife, and they will become one flesh" (Genesis 2:24). Here, we see a new relational priority is established. God was setting forth a principle for dealing with marital problems and pressures—like in-law tensions and misunderstandings—that the rest of us would face. And imagine, the Lord gave this instruction to Adam and Eve—who had no parents!

It's so important to realize that when you marry you have established a new family, apart from the family you knew as a child. Although one does not replace or give up the parental family, unless we loosen the ties with our parents enough to form new bonds with our mate, we cannot have a healthy marriage.

My eldest son lived in our home until the day he got married. I took him breakfast in bed the day of his wedding and even packed his suitcase for his honeymoon. That evening I turned him over to another woman.

Maybe it was just the grace of God, but this was very easy for me. However, I realize this is more difficult for some. Adjustments take time. Patience, therefore, is essential on both sides. When you're first married, for example, you not only want his parents' acceptance, but his parents' approval as well.

I try to let my daughters-in-law and my son-in-law know how much I approve of them and how much I appreciate them. I try to encourage them and tell them how thankful I am for them—just as my mother-in-law did to me.

— ❧ —

I know a young girl whose in-laws were a bit demanding.

Remember: You're on the Same Team

When problems occur in your marriage, remind yourselves you're on the same team. It's not you and your parents against him and his parents. If your parents are trying to divide you, simply stand firm together remembering that your own marriage is the priority relationship.

—Susan

For example, they expected to have a say in her decorating decisions; and they expected her and her husband to be at their home every Sunday for dinner. Of course, this began to upset my young friend, and rightly so. However, I tried to help her mellow a bit, and pointed out, "This is a strong, united family and you're going to have to take it easy. *Slowly* change these traditions to allow time for your own. But do it with sweetness and graciousness so that you don't cause a battle between you and your in-laws or between you and your husband." That made sense to her and she became less intent on having her own way, avoiding a lot of conflict with her new family.

Now, some time later, things are improving slowly. I asked her recently how things were going. "Oh better," she replied. "My in-laws were out of town all summer!" We both laughed.

As my young friend is learning, the in-law relationship generally improves as years go by. The tensions of the early years usually lessen over time. I have another friend whose parents didn't accept her husband. They were angry the two married and would have very little to do with them. However, over the years, the in-laws came to consider their son-in-law as much a part of the family as their daughter.

That says a lot for the son-in-law. He was able to sweetly work his way into their hearts. If he had reacted harshly and pulled his wife away, love, acceptance, and appreciation would never have developed. The Bible reminds us to let our sweet reasonableness be known to all—in-laws included.

Conflict Resolution: Show Respect

We are also reminded in Scripture to treat our in-laws with respect. This *does not* mean we have to obey them or agree with them. Rather, we must respect the position they hold in our lives. They are, after all, not only our new parents, but our children's grandparents as well.

Such a show of respect can, of course, be difficult— especially when we find ourselves in disagreement over some matter. And yet, politeness and consideration should be our approach at all times.

You Really Do Need Each Other

Jealousy can cause in-law problems. Instead of being jealous, work on being thankful that your husband has a family that cares about what happens to their son. Try to enjoy and celebrate what is outstanding in your husband's family: his mother's cooking, his father's skills, their traditions, their ethnic backgrounds. If you can learn as much as possible about these things, it will help you to not feel threatened by them—and it will free your husband to learn to appreciate the uniqueness of your own family.

The struggle to create healthy extended family relationships is worth the effort. When it gets difficult, don't drop out. Kids need grandparents and aunts and uncles for a sense of perspective. You need roots, too. It's worth the struggle—you really do need each other.

—Gloria

That said, there nevertheless will be confrontation from time to time. If you have a problem, the best way to deal with it is to get all persons involved together for a talk. The ideal would be for your husband to take the lead in this delicate interaction— sticking up for you and helping you tell your in-laws how their behavior makes you feel. With such a unified effort, you and your husband can effectively communicate the fact that you are a "team," and that problems are addressed together.

Some people accept this kind of confrontation better than others. But you may have to stick to your convictions until the message is heard. And remember: be sweetly firm—and patient.

If your in-laws will not release control and you want to avoid continual battles, you may need to remove yourself from the situation. (I have even known of extreme cases where couples have had to leave town!) The important thing is, you've got to be able to establish your own foundation as a couple. You can't expect to grow in your own relationship if you've got an overwhelming battle with in-laws going on over an extended period of time.

And don't forget to pray. I was talking to a friend who's been married thirty years—a gracious Christian woman who's mother-in-law has been continuously hurtful to her and her family. At one point the mother-in-law went so far as to accuse my friend of a very heinous sin in front of her whole family at a Thanksgiving dinner. All of my friend's children and her grand-children were furious, and they were going to go up to Great-Grandmother and really blast her when my friend stopped them and said, "No, let's not do that. Let's pray for her, and then let's go and ask her what we can do to help her today. Let's treat her with love."

Sad to say, that situation has not gotten much better. But my friend has earned the love and respect of her husband and children.

She also continues to pray, "Lord, show me creative ways of showing love to my mother-in-law."

Make It Happen

1. Tell your husband what kind of relationship you'd like to have with his parents. Then hear him out regarding your parents. Compare your expectations and determine what steps need to be taken to bring about the relationships you desire.

2. Do something nice for your in-laws. Take them something special from the bakery, send them a funny family photograph, or

simply call to say hello. Small gestures like these will build friendships.

3. Try to compromise more often than your husband. If you both had that mindset, your marriage would be a prime example of sacrificial love. Be willing to put your husband first as Scripture instructs (Philippians 2).

Chapter 4

CAN OUR MARRIAGE HANDLE CHILDREN?
Gloria Gaither

I s *anybody* ever ready to be a parent?

A new father once told me, "Everybody said having a baby was going to alter my schedule. But this baby has totally changed my life!" Truer words were never spoken. And the truth of the matter is, that child will continue to change this father's life—as an infant, as a toddler, as a teenager, as an adult.

As the mother of two daughters and one son, I can say unequivocally that children stretch and pull at a marriage. They provide both its greatest joys and greatest frustrations. They expose our weaknesses and, in turn, develop our strengths. Children challenge us to grow not only as parents, but as Christians.

Once we make the decision to have children, our lives will never be the same. That's why we need to realistically recognize the demands of parenting before a baby keeps us up for two or three years straight, and there is no energy for sex and intimacy, and we're too tired to think, and are no longer charming because we haven't read a real book in months.

Ironically, even with all the books, seminars, and friendly advice available today, I'm convinced none of us can be fully prepared for the surprises God has in store for us as mothers and fathers. However, in considering the "am I ready" question, I think there are a couple of fundamental questions that need to be addressed.

First, are you expecting children to improve your marriage? You should not have children to fix something that's broken, to bring you and your husband closer together, to make you love each other more, or simply to make your husband stay home more.

Having children does what money and age do. It only makes you "more." If you're generous and kind, money makes you more so. If you're selfish and greedy, money makes you more so. In the same way, children intensify and bring out the things that are good in us, and they expose the things that are bad in us.

Second, are you struggling with some unresolved emotional issues that might make it difficult for you to parent successfully? If you get angry easily, for instance, it would be good to get some counseling before becoming a parent. Find out where the rage is coming from. Children will bring out your weaknesses. They may scream all night, they may have temper tantrums, or be physically frail. Parenting requires emotional stamina. I would advise couples to deal with the worst in themselves before the children arrive.

Someone who has come from an abusive background or who has had a very unhappy childhood may have more to work through than other people. If you're from an unhappy background, besides getting professional help, spend time with a mature, adjusted couple who have children. Watch how they relate to their kids. Observe how they treat each other. How do they deal with the unexpected? Be honest with this couple and say, "We aren't from happy homes and we need to be around a healthy family so we have a picture of what our home can be like."

Our Checks and Balances

While I've focused on some of the difficulties of parenthood, the truth is that children are incredibly "worth it." I have learned more about grace from my children than from anyone else. Over and over they forgive me and love me when I least deserve it.

In a spiritual sense, kids become a check and balance. My oldest daughter, Suzanne, for example, is incredibly just. Even as a child she would challenge the "fairness" of certain decisions or pinpoint unhealthy attitudes in me or Bill. Now, at this stage of our lives, I actively seek out her advice on issues that I'm dealing with. I ask her if I'm being fair, knowing that if I'm not, she'll tell me!

> ### Never Ready, Ever Ready
> *We're never really ready to be parents. In fact, once you've had children you know you were not ready. I've been a parent for almost twenty-eight years, and at times I still feel like a failure. That's where dependence on the Lord comes in. We accept by faith that children are a blessing from him. We see this all the way through Scripture. Rely on God for the strength you need.*
>
> *—Gigi*

Then there's our middle child, Amy—the compassionate one—the child who, growing up, was reluctant to accept that people were ever truly evil through and through. She even asked me if Satan could be saved if we prayed real hard!

Amy is the child I go to for advice on how to bring love into situations in which I feel I've been unfairly treated or hurt.

And last, there's Benjy, our youngest. The prophet! Hard edged. Black and white. You know where he stands. And what does he bring to me? The challenge of having to know where I stand and to defend why I believe the things I believe.

All three of our children have taught Bill and me more theology than we could ever have learned from a hundred seminary courses. And they've made that theology practical. Pious platitudes are meaningless without the appropriate actions. And there's no one more likely than a child to pick up any inconsistencies.

If you feel you are ready to love a child, then trust the future of that child to the Lord. God didn't send Jesus to earth at a time when all the conflicts of the world were resolved and everyone was at peace. My own birth came when our country was at war—three months after the Japanese bombed Pearl Harbor. There's never been a good time to bring children into the world.

The song "Because He Lives" was written when we were expecting our son, Benjy, at the end of the sixties. I was afraid to have a child with the world like it was—the racial tensions, drugs, and the Vietnam War.

Bill and I thought, "Who in their right minds would bring a child into a world like this? If it's like this now, what will it be like in eighteen years when he has to face adulthood?"

But we came to realize that we don't find the courage to face the future because the world is stable; we face the future because Jesus lives. Resurrection in the face of death is a reality of life in him. When Benjy was born—so perfect, so special, so innocent— a song was born as well:

No Perfect Parents

If you are part of the Baby Boomer generation, you're used to being prepared for the things you attempt to do. You don't want to do anything unless you know you can succeed. But I don't think success is all that important to God. I think God just wants us to grow in him. It's incredible that he's willing to entrust us with some little people to raise. And we need to know we're going to fail, but failure need not be devastating. Failure can be positive. We learn a lot from our failures.

I would say if you have a desire to have children, and you're open to God teaching you through them and helping you learn how to parent, then go for it!

—Susan

> How sweet to hold our newborn baby,
> And feel the pride and joy he gives.
> But greater still, the calm assurance,
> This child can face uncertain days because He lives.

Make It Happen

1. Try to determine what is holding you back from having children. There may be some fears or some doubts that you and your husband can work through together.

2. Look at the families in your church. Are there one or two that you would like to model your family after? Tell them you'd like to spend time with them and learn from their example.

3. If you're concerned about financially affording a child, talk to a financial counselor and find out what adjustments you need to make to your financial game plan.

4. Children require sacrifice. Before you have children, be sure you're ready to give up whatever is necessary for their good. Could you leave your job? Are you willing to move to a more affordable area or one more suited to raising a family? Can you give up the bulk of your personal space and privacy? As you face these challenges, remind yourself of Gloria's words: "Children are incredibly worth it."

Chapter 5

HOW DO I FIND TIME FOR MY HUSBAND AND MY KIDS?
Susan Alexander Yates

 remember lying on the couch one stormy afternoon feeling completely overwhelmed. The phone had been ringing constantly: a request to do some volunteer work; a request to bake cookies for a bake sale; a request to help out with Sunday school. I felt like the tree being blown every-which-way by the wind. There were just so many opportunities and demands on my time that I was losing track of when to say no and when to say yes.

I've often wished I could add six more hours to my kitchen clock to squeeze everything in. However, God gives each of us only twenty-four hours a day, and experience has shown me that what really makes a difference in handling a hectic life is a heart knowledge of the biblical priorities of God, husband, and children. I'll admit, such an approach is hardly revolutionary. And it always amazes me how basic, yet perfect, God's ways are. But I've found that when I *really* apply God's priorities to my life, it truly revolutionizes how I manage my time.

God Centered Priorities

To keep my number one priority just that, I need to make time daily for the Lord. I try to take at least thirty minutes in the morning simply to study the Bible and to pray. I can't say I succeed all of the time. I am constantly striving to understand my priorities and keep them in line. There are times when several days go by and I haven't found time for God first. Soon I begin to notice how I can't quite seem to balance the time demands. Johnny may not get the listening ear he needs while the kids do, or vice versa.

To make time for our first priority, we need to avoid thinking that once the kids are older, we'll have more time for prayer and Bible study. Frankly, I was more disciplined when my children were young—I had to be. I was desperate to be in the Word, so I worked to find time five minutes here, five minutes there. But when the kids grew older, and I found my schedule more flexible, I also found it easier to postpone my devotions to some later time. And "later" would never come.

Today, I find that if I don't meet with the Lord in the morning I don't do it at all. But you need to find a time that's right for you. Through prayer, reading my Bible, and occasionally using devotional classics like Oswald Chamber's *My Utmost for His Highest*, I am reminded of God's priorities for me. Then, when opportunities to use my time are presented, I can choose my involvements wisely.

Husband Before Children

Once our first priority is in place, "loving the Lord your God with all your heart, soul, strength, and mind," we then need to focus on another great commandment—"love your neighbor as yourself." And who is your nearest neighbor? Your husband.

Genesis 2:20-25 describes the mystical and permanent characteristics of marriage—namely that two have come together as one for a lifetime. Realistically, our children will live with Johnny and me for a brief season, eighteen to twenty years. However, God willing, Johnny will be with me the rest of my life.

While most of us know this truth, few of us live as if that knowledge has gone to our hearts. We live in a child-oriented society. In fact, we so cater to our children that we forget the husband/wife relationship is more important.

I'll never forget how clearly this truth was proven by a Christian family I know that almost fell apart. The mother's whole life was thrown into the kids. Whatever they needed or wanted, they got. Their needs were top priority. Worse yet, she used the children and their needs

> ## Simplifying Life
> In our home we told the children, "You can choose one activity a semester. And that's it. You can't be involved in three or four different activities." This simplified life tremendously.
>
> —Gigi

to call the shots in the marriage. For instance, if her husband wanted to take her out for the evening, her reply most often was, "But we just can't. Billy really wants me to take him to ball practice tonight and watch." Compounding this, she heaped guilt on her husband by adding, "Billy needs me. You don't care about him."

This woman would have been surprised to realize that she was subtly manipulating her husband. It was unintentional. Her mothering instincts were simply on "overdrive."

Eventually, a distance developed between the couple. They seldom talked and, when they did, most conversations revolved around the kids. Fortunately, the couple went to counseling. During the months in counseling the wife learned her behavior was not only hurting the marriage but her children as well. By making her children her number one priority, she was unwittingly making them more self-centered. She did not realize the subtle message: Children come before marriage. If we want our children to have strong marriages, they need to live in a home where the marriage relationship is high priority.

There is a little bit of this woman in all mothers. Most of us will do anything for our children. We don't want to disappoint them. After all they need us—they're only kids! But kids have got to learn to wait if we want them to grow into mature adults.

A child's security is based not on how much his parents

love him, but on how much his parents love each other. Even though they may complain outwardly, your children are genuinely pleased that you make your marriage a priority.

— ❦ —

We need to cultivate our relationship with our husband from day one. Before Johnny and I were married, a wise friend suggested we take one night a week and go out. I thought it was a bit silly at the time, but we did it. Johnny was in seminary and I was working full-time—we had a demanding schedule. Nonetheless, we went out for coffee one night a week. We didn't go with other friends, we simply went out, the two of us. Alone.

It was important that we fostered that discipline early. That made it easier to continue once we had children and life became more complex. Sometimes we had to get two babysitters to handle all our kids. But that weekly "date" helped us continue cultivating our relationship. I knew we would have one time each week when we would be together. We did not necessarily talk about anything heavy; we simply enjoyed each other's company.

Taking Time to Parent

It's true we live in a child-centered society. But there are also a lot of parents neglecting their children. Sometimes there's the temptation to get our children so involved in school activities that we don't have to parent them. We relieve our guilt by running them to softball practice.

I don't think it's always the family's fault. Our culture tends to measure how well our kids are doing by how many activities they're involved in. Parents try to show they are doing a good job by saying, "My son's in soccer," or "My daughter is in ballet." But we have to take time to parent. My kids would much rather have me be home and having a hot dog roast than have the opportunity to say their mother's on some important board or committee— and never home!

—Gloria

With the kids older, we now go out every Friday for breakfast. Or I should say we try to. There are times we fall prey to the tyranny of the urgent, and let this special time slip away. However, our commitment to this time alone remains strong, because we are committed to knowing each other better.

If going out is financially difficult, be creative! Set a table in the living room in front of the fireplace and create an in-house restaurant. We have done that—we call it the Blonde Fox Inn, named after a favorite country inn of ours—and the fact that we're a family of blondes. We told the kids this was our date night and they couldn't come in the living room. The big kids put the little ones to bed. Those evenings were as special as if we'd gone out to an expensive restaurant.

It's also important to get away overnight. A change of scenery does wonders. If you are a two-career couple, you may have more funds to spend on some really exciting things. But it doesn't have to be an elaborate trip. Once we went to a motel three-quarters of a mile from our house just for the night. We had a nice dinner, a comfortable room, and the pleasure of uninterrupted sleep. Then Johnny got up and went to work the next day. It was a short but valuable break.

It helps to have a regular get-away weekend on your calendar—even if it's just once a year. My brother-in-law is an accountant and the tax season is especially demanding. By the time April 15 comes, he literally needs to sleep for two or three days. But he and his wife plan to go away, just the two of them, about a week later. During the weeks my sister rarely sees her husband, she keeps reminding herself of the special get-away they have planned.

Sometimes you can piggyback on business trips. We have a friend who will occasionally take his wife or a child with him and stay over an extra day in the city where he has business. Or he'll use bonus airline tickets for a special trip. There are lots of ways to get away from home.

This all sounds great, you say, but we don't have the money. It is wise to look at your financial priorities. Over the long haul, it is better to invest in relationships than in things. We'd rather spend money on family vacations—or a weekend getaway for just the two of us—than on a chair that would finally finish off our living room. Sometimes it helps to ask: What do my spending habits tell me about our real priorities?

And Now the Kids . . .

All that said, it's obviously important to balance couple time with kid time. We may realize, for example, that a child has a real need; say a recital at school where your presence is really crucial. Perhaps it falls on the night that you and your husband had planned to be together, yet you know it would be best if you attended the recital instead. There's got to be some flexibility.

Both parents also need to find time to spend one-on-one with each of their children. One thing that has worked well for us is periodically pulling the kids out of school to have lunch with either Mom or Dad. The kids enjoy the change of pace. And their principals haven't minded one bit.

—— ❦ ——

It's a fallacy to think that "things" will eventually calm down, making priorities easier to balance. With almost five teenagers in our home, I'm daily finding that things rarely calm down—they simply get more complicated. That's why I need to stay alert of what's happening with my relationships and see that they truly reflect God's perfect priorities for my life.

Do I get frustrated? You bet! But God has given me a lifetime to work on this holy balancing act, and ample amounts of his grace to help me get through those times when everything seems to be up for grabs. He is always ready to forgive me when I blow it and to pick me up yet another time when I fail. I'm learning to appreciate the "small" blessings: a particularly moving time in the Word; an hour alone with my husband, and an appreciative kiss from a child, these remind me that all things are possible through him who loves me!

Teach Your Children Well
Karen Heffner

Parents usually don't hesitate to help their children make wise choices when they are selecting a college or a career. But there is another decision most young adults make that unfortunately often gets minimal parental attention—the selection of a life mate. However, children naturally view their parents' marriage as a model, and can be relatively uninhibited about asking questions on marriage and family matters. What better environment is there for communication?

Some points to consider:

Be honest in sharing marriage struggles. One woman confessed that she was devastated when her new husband displayed an angry outburst toward her while they were still on their honeymoon. She had grown up in a home where her parents apparently had never exchanged a cross word in front of their children. Conflict in marriage is inevitable and needn't be entirely negative. It can be used as a springboard to discuss matters like accepting differences and asking for and granting forgiveness.

Even if a marriage has ended in divorce, parents still can have a positive influence on their children's marriage—if they are candid about their failures and share what they've learned. Perhaps the truth is that "We were too young, I'm afraid, and we simply didn't work at understanding each other like we should have," or "I know now that it's very important that a husband and wife can share their faith in God."

Everyday family events can trigger conversations

about marriage: the family is invited to a wedding, a friend gets a divorce, a child asks how Mommy and Daddy met. If we seize the moment, we may find ourselves talking about what it means to "fall in love." That may lead to a discussion of the ways a man shows he loves his family, or character traits that are attractive in a spouse.

The parent who has consistently thought about and prayed for a child's future marriage is in a good position to spot traits that might hinder her child's developing good habits.

Children whose parents consistently hold up marriage as a high calling are more likely to enter their own marriages with a solid commitment to their vows. And when problems arise, they may have an easier time seeking counsel.

When families have talked about marriage "academically," children will be less apt to think their parents are meddling when they bring it up specifically concerning someone their child is dating. Some prior "practice" is good when it comes to emotional discussions.

Gear discussions to the child's ability to understand. That way, he—and you—will not feel overwhelmed, threatened, or frustrated. It is well to remember, however, that children may have more knowledge—even if it has been gathered in bits and pieces from sources outside the home—than we expect. The most important benefit of keeping communication lines open may be to have the opportunity to dispel untruths and encourage healthy, godly attitudes about relationships between the sexes.

From Today's Christian Woman
(May/June 1989)

Make It Happen

1. Evaluate your schedule. What activities could you eliminate to make more time for your husband?

2. Ask your husband what he considers to be "a really good time." Plan a special evening doing what he suggests. This will communicate how much you value him and your relationship.

3. Look at your calendar and find a weekend you and your husband could spend together. Begin planning and saving now to make it happen.

4. Develop the habit of showing your husband affection in front of your children. Do what's comfortable for you—maybe holding hands while you watch television. These small actions will show your kids that their parents are still in love, a very reassuring concept.

Chapter 6

HOW MUCH SHOULD I EXPECT MY HUSBAND TO DO AROUND THE HOUSE?
Gigi Graham Tchividjian

y daughter, Berdjette, has a very demanding job as a manager of a resort hotel. Her work days easily go ten to twelve hours and there are many nights she literally comes home exhausted. Her husband, David, works mostly out of the home as a financial consultant, and sweetly does his share of housework.

However, one day Berdjette called me and said, "Mama, David was a bit down one day this week, and that's not like him. So I crawled up in his lap and asked, 'What's the matter honey?' When he said nothing, I put my arms around him and said, 'Yes, there is. Tell me what's the matter.'

"Finally he said, 'There's not one clean pair of underwear or socks in my whole drawer.' "

My daughter kissed her husband, then they laughed over his "predicament," got up, and spent the rest of the evening doing laundry together.

I told this story to another young friend who's been married only a short time. And her reaction was not anything like my daughter's. "I'd say, you're big enough to do your own laundry," my friend said. "I'm not your mother."

These two responses to David's "dilemma" remind me again of the varying attitudes with which we approach all responsibilities in marriage—especially parenting and house-work. No matter if you work full-time or are at home full-time, the rub of children and housework is ever present in marriage. And the potential for conflict can bring tension to even the quietest home.

Grating Expectations

A few years ago, the lines of responsibility were more clearly drawn. But now with so many women working outside the home, roles and responsibilities have changed. Despite all the talk about men being more involved in the home, statistics prove that women still do most of the housework. (Although from my "unscientific" observations, younger men are more apt to pitch in and help than older men.) And, as most of us know, an unequal division of labor, real or perceived, can lead to frustration and resentment.

So can we really hope to have a husband who leaps to do the dishes each night? Or throws in a load of laundry on his way past the washing machine?

For me, the answer comes in expectations—both in what my husband should and shouldn't do around the house, as well as how tough I am on myself regarding how the house should look.

This is where Stephan has taught me a lot about tradeoffs—that is, learning how one choice dictates another. For instance, I could have a spotless house (my personal preference) but I have learned the tradeoff is total exhaustion (and with seven children, total frustration). I wouldn't get books written either, and the children would be miserable because I'd be on their backs all the time. The alternative is to have a less than perfect house, with the tradeoff being a happier home and a more productive me. I'm hard on myself, but I'm learning to see it's okay to lower my expectations a little. A few years ago if I saw a bit of lint on the carpet I would have jumped up immediately to pick it up. Now I can say, "Oh, I'll just leave it or get it later."

Along with getting your personal expectations in line with reality, it helps to bring those expectations you have for your husband down a notch or two. Sometimes we get irritated with our husbands because they don't help with the "obvious" tasks. And yet, these tasks aren't always "obvious" to our husband—a lot of men honestly don't see what needs to be done around the house. A wife may need to be direct and tell her husband specific tasks he can do to help her, such as grocery shopping, helping the children with their homework, or vacuuming the carpet.

Follow Through

We may ask our husbands to do specific tasks, but how do we inspire them to follow through? The motivational methods we have to choose from are limited. We can nag—but from my experience that won't bring any long-term results. Or we can lay on the guilt, like I sometimes do unintentionally. I'll say "Oh, so you're in here watching the news in the bedroom? Well, I'm still cleaning the kitchen." But needless to say, that kind of remark only adds to the tension and rarely brings about change.

Plan Ahead

Once, when we went on vacation with two babies, we learned the importance of teamwork. Johnny and I were both burned out from our youth ministry. He had his vision of "vacation equals rest." He would get up in the morning and go have this wonderful, long quiet time. Meanwhile, I was wiped because I had been up most of the night with one of the babies. I wanted rest and he wanted rest.

Before long, my husband realized he needed to help me. We worked out a schedule in which we each took care of the children for two hours to give the other person time alone.

That experience began to show me that we need to anticipate problems or awkward situations. The next time we got ready to go on vacation, we talked through the tensions and planned how we were going to deal with them. I began applying the "plan ahead" principle to home life, too. I'd look at the week ahead and try to anticipate where I would need help. I'd then ask Johnny and the children to get involved.

—Susan

A more positive approach is to simply let go. Years ago, Stephan had the habit of placing his clothes on the rocking chair in our bedroom every night instead of hanging them up. Then I would usually hang them up the next morning. I finally decided to let his clothes sit there and see what happened. The pile got so high that the rocker fell over backwards. He's hung his clothes up ever since. And I didn't have to say a word.

Also, let me encourage you to get in the habit of carefully noting—and appreciating—what your husband *does do* around the house. Does he maintain the cars? Does he do household repairs or work in the yard? We need to consider these things before deciding "he just doesn't do enough!" Maybe he does more than you think—but in his own way and in his own time.

Who's Helping Whom?

Early on in our marriage, Bill had his aunt help care for our home and children. Three days a week she would take care of a thousand details—from calling the chimney sweep to changing the beds. She was a widow, and found the crazy traffic in our home a welcome antidote for loneliness. This arrangement, therefore, met a need in her life, too.

—Gloria

The best approach, however, is to openly communicate. Work out a mutually agreed upon division of labor. Remember, your health and mental well-being are at stake as well as the atmosphere of the home.

Discuss the situation and the need to come up with an equitable split of responsibilities. And if that can't be done, then suggest that the family budget might be reorganized to include money for some outside help.

In dividing up responsibilities, it's also helpful for husbands and wives to figure out their preferences. Stephan works with a man who loves to cook. So this man has taken over that responsibility in his home. He does the grocery shopping, the cooking, the clean up—everything from start to finish. And he loves it. So if you know your husband has particular gifts or certain things he enjoys doing, start there.

Not all husbands will be open to renegotiating household responsibilities. Some will not want to help at all. But don't be discouraged—there are alternatives. If you have children, then teach them to help. Explain that chores are part of the responsibility and privilege of living in their home. Don't ask them to do jobs that are beyond their abilities. A four-year-old can put his dirty clothes in the hamper and empty waste baskets, but don't ask him to dry the dishes. That will only frustrate him. Begin by assigning simple tasks. As a child masters each task, challenge him with another. And remember not to let them slack off. My kids are often called back from their friends' houses if they forget to do their chores.

Once you've got the children used to the idea of helping around the house, you might approach your husband with the idea of supervising the children's chores. That would be a way he could help with a minimum investment of his time. And it would be a great encouragement to you.

Sometimes it really helps me when I'm tired or have had a busy day to have Stephan come in and say, "Okay, kids, you two clear the table. You sweep the floor. You empty the dishwasher. You feed the dog. Gigi, you come sit down with me in the living room."

While the option of outside help may sound prohibitive from a financial perspective, with a little creative thinking you'd be surprised at the number of feasible options available.

For instance, when my kids were younger, we couldn't afford full-time help. We instead had a series of young girls, ages eighteen to twenty, stay with us and help out—girls who wanted to be away from home for a while yet wanted a home environment. It was a great help to me, but they also benefited since it was an excellent opportunity for them to learn about housekeeping, family life, and child care.

If you live in a college town, consider hiring a student to tackle some of the big jobs that hang over your head like washing windows or cleaning the oven. I no longer need full-time help, but with my busy schedule I still have part-time household help. And just knowing that somebody is helping to clean the house takes pressure off me.

You might also talk to your friends and see if you could share housekeeping. I heard of two women who worked together on Saturdays, alternating between their two homes. They knew their homes would get a thorough cleaning every two weeks and all they would have to do is basic maintenance in the meantime. Working together was easier, and gave them time to talk and build their friendship.

I've even heard of women working out a job exchange. Babysit for each other to provide uninterrupted time for errands or chores. Still other women trade off specific jobs. One woman likes to cook, so she bakes her friend a week's worth of meals while her friend cleans the house.

———

Like with so much of marriage, the key to "job sharing" is clear communication. We need to talk patiently and lovingly to our mates about our frustrations. And once those frustrations are out on the table, we can together develop a strategy in which household duties can be dealt with—with our goal being the creation of a home our family loves to come home to.

Train Up a . . . Spouse?

Elizabeth Cody Newenhuyse

It never fails. I come home from work, hang up my coat, and drop my purse on a chair. Then I go in the kitchen—and wipe the stove. The stove always has coffee stains on it, because my husband, who works at home and drinks "decaf" all day, doesn't understand about wiping things. He's pretty good about picking up after himself. I don't have to contend with a trail of discarded clothes or a clutter of week-old newspapers.

But wiping is something else. Fritz went to Harvard, but he never learned that liquid spills become solid spills if not wiped immediately.

I've tried educating him. I've yelled, I've cajoled, I've even gotten out the SOS pad and scrubbed. No change. I've decided it's a basic hormonal difference: Men don't scrub stoves, because they literally don't see the spill. So rather than nag, I quietly wipe.

We women have a "fix-it" instinct. We go on diets, rearrange furniture, advise friends, remind our children to brush before bedtime. And we secretly believe we can train our husbands to wipe the counter, or close the curtain when they shower, or close anything, for that matter.

Ah, opening and closing. A group of my men and women friends recently had an animated luncheon discussion about spouses (like mine) who leave doors and drawers open. One man said his wife pulls out their dresser drawers so far the chest actually falls over. My husband leaves his drawers open just a bit, but always with a piece of sock or sweater sticking out. It drives me crazy. The outlook, however, is not promising—we've been married more than ten years, and if he hasn't learned by now . . .

"Learned" is the key word here. It implies that I'm trying to teach Fritz something. But Proverbs 22 does not say, "Train up a husband in the way he should go."

Husbands, I have concluded, will "go" whichever way they want. You can train a dog or a horse. You can train a rosebush to climb a trellis. But I cannot train my beloved to sort laundry correctly. Fritz crams our washing machine to the brim—red towels, blue jeans, white (well, they were once) slips. Then he stuffs it all into the dryer. I have patiently explained to him, "My Dear, clothes dry by the circulation of warm air around the various garments, and by the free movement of clothing within the drum. Hence the instructions, 'Tumble dry.'" His reply? "Well, do you want to do the wash?"

Touché!

From Today's Christian Woman
(March/April 1989)

Make It Happen

1. Before you talk to your husband about sharing the work load, determine if you're hurt because he is being insensitive to you, or if you're frustrated because you're overworked. These are separate, though related, issues that will require different resolutions.

2. As Gigi suggested, take inventory of the tasks you like to do around the house and those you don't. Ask your husband to do the same. This might help you determine who will do what chores. It will also help you know what kind of job exchange you could work out if you decide to approach your friends for help.

3. Try different systems of keeping up with your housework. For instance, find out if you prefer doing a little bit each day or tackling the whole house on Saturday. But make sure you keep up. If you get too far behind, it can become a frustation that, in turn, can lead to tension.

4. Simplify your lifestyle. The less you have to take care of, the less time it will require to maintain it.

THE "C" WORD

S o much has been written about communication and marriage that the more cynical among us might think that little else needs to be said.

Wrong!

Communication—or lack of communication between wife and husband—remains the number one problem in marriage today, hands down. How to get beyond such "infotalk" as the weather or schedules remains a serious hurdle that couples— Christian and non-Christian—almost universally need work overcoming.

That's why in the following chapters, Gigi and Susan speak passionately out of their own experiences concerning the importance of "talk time," and offer some practical tips on how to make that one-on-one time work for you.

As Susan says, good communication doesn't just happen. It takes time, effort, and dedication to the task at hand. It evolves over time as two people gradually become more vulnerable and more willing to share their deeper selves with the other. Therefore, says Susan, "We can either resent the communications challenge—clam up and silently withdraw from our spouse—or we can see it as an opportunity for God's grace to flow through us and draw us more intimately together."

Chapter 7

HOW CAN I DEEPEN THE COMMUNICATION BETWEEN MY HUSBAND AND MYSELF?
Susan Alexander Yates

here have been times in my marriage where I've asked Johnny about his day and only gotten the facts—who he met with and a few of the problems he encountered. But what I really wanted to know was how he felt about his day. When this happens, I'm sure I feel like most women—a little frustrated that the communication in our marriage didn't seem to reach a level of real sharing.

Experience has shown me that women are *generally* more aware of the need for deeper communication—yet that doesn't mean men aren't. It's just that for some men, sharing their feelings doesn't come as naturally or as easily as it does for women. Fortunately, with a little work, you can help your husband become comfortable with sharing not just the details of his day but his thoughts and feelings about each day as well.

But I'll be honest. When it comes to keeping the channels of communication open in the Yates's home, I've learned there are no magic words to make my husband "open up." Rather, communication—good communication, that is—takes time and effort. It takes planning. It takes work! But after twenty-plus years of marriage, I can honestly say the payback's been well-worth the effort.

From the times Johnny and I have really tapped into one another's feelings, we have seen a noticeable growth in our knowledge of each other. And from this knowledge, we have seen our marriage relationship strengthen and a greater sense of intimacy develop.

Communication and the Marriage Covenant

Building good communication into a marriage, those times when you share more than tonight's dinner menu or the kids' schedules, does not *begin* with setting aside "X" minutes of quality talk time a day or implementing any number of other good, practical tips offered in numerous marriage books. Rather, effective communication begins with how you view your marriage.

Our cultural mindset today sees marriage as anything but permanent. If there are any flaws, any disappointments, any expectations not met, I am free to leave to pursue "perfection" elsewhere. Little wonder that one of the most popular seminars in Washington, D.C., today is on how to write prenuptial contracts!

But marriage is a covenant relationship—not a contract. By covenant, I mean marriage is viewed as a *permanent* commitment of two people. As it's stated in Genesis 2:24, "A man will leave his father and mother, and be united to his wife and they will become one flesh." Viewing marriage in such a way does two things for husband-wife communication.

First, it gives us security and freedom. In our success-oriented society, we expect instant breakthroughs and solutions. But we do our husbands—and ourselves—a disservice if we bring such skewed thinking into our marriages. Under covenant, I have a lifetime to learn how to bond together as one to my husband. Under covenant, I have a lifetime to discover how best to communicate with this man. The "I do" I said on my wedding day was not the *culmination* of a relationship, but the *beginning* of a new commitment. It's a commitment to work on my relationship with my husband for the rest of my life.

Second, covenant provides us with the challenge to grow in our marriage. After all, if I'm committed to Johnny for the long haul, I can either live in solitude, emotionally divorcing myself from him, or I can build my friendship with him by working on communication and continuing to discover new things about him.

In a sense, then, covenant forces me either to talk or to resign myself to a marriage that is physically, emotionally, and spiritually shallow. It encourages me to know my husband—and my husband to know me. And it gives us a lifetime to grow together in deep friendship.

— ❧ —

Viewing marriage as covenant is foundational to effective communication. Yet there is another principle to remember when tackling the question of communication. And it is one, like the understanding of marriage as covenant, that has been challenged quite a bit lately. Namely, that men and women *are* different.

Couple Mode

In the evenings, rather than barreling into another problem when you've been solving problems all day, try to get out of the office mode or out of the traffic mode or out of the water softener mode or the PTA mode, and get into the couple mode. Zero in on your mate and on yourself. Think, "We are two married people. We love each other." "A walk in the park would do us good. We'll take a cup of coffee." Things like that will get you back into a mode where you're thinking "home."

—Gloria

I'm not referring to specific roles or abilities. Rather, I'm referring to the mysterious way God has made us; the sensitivities he has built into each one of us.

And while there are exceptions to every "rule," experience has shown me again and again that one key difference between men and women is a woman's greater capacity for relationships and communication. Consequently, we may be expecting a level of openness from our spouse that is unreasonable, or at least uncomfortable for him.

It's interesting to notice the different communication styles of men and women. Men, for example, often prefer to talk while doing something. We women can sit and talk for hours—not so with most men. Johnny and I get together with two couples twice a year. During the weekend, we laugh, we pray, and we share. And it's interesting—the three of us women will curl up in front of the fireplace with a cup of tea and talk deeply by the hour. The men go out and talk while they chop wood.

I have a friend who is married to a painfully shy, quiet spouse. In the evening, after they get their children settled doing homework, they will walk briskly for about two or three miles. He's more likely to reveal what he's thinking and feeling while they walk because the focus isn't communication, it's exercise.

The Right Atmosphere

The more tense I am from my day, the less Stephan feels like opening up when he comes home in the evening. He just feels like going to his room and getting away from everything. I still think that the major responsibility for atmosphere rests on the woman's shoulders. Whether it's fair or not, it's just a fact. I think the children react much more to the mother's moods, and I think the husband does, too.

—*Gigi*

Creating a Mood for Communication

Once we take into account some of the basic differences between men and women, we are then in a position to take some practical steps to building better communication in our marriage. And since women often recognize the need for deeper communication, the responsibility for taking those beginning steps usually falls to us.

I vividly remember this being the case when Johnny and I moved to Virginia to assume his first senior pastorate. We were in that season of life when our children were always underfoot (we had five kids seven and under!); and between meeting their needs, adjusting to a new community, and Johnny establishing himself at the church, we were both zombies. But worse, we were losing touch with each other. Johnny was at the church most nights. And by the time he'd get home, his kids *and* his wife would usually be in bed. Needless to say, I was frustrated and so was he.

Finally, I shared my frustrations with him. I felt that our conversation had become purely functional—information, dates, events. We no longer took time to get beneath the surface and discuss how we were really feeling about all that was happening in our lives.

I told Johnny: "I want to know what's going on in your life because I love you. I want to feel a part of you."

That was a turning point for us. We initiated a tradition called "tea time." As soon as Johnny got home, we would sit for about fifteen minutes, drink tea, and talk. This was our time to share how we felt about ourselves and how our days had gone. We tried to share more than surface conversation. The kids were allowed to be with us but they could not talk. Usually after a few minutes they would get bored and find ways to entertain themselves. Afterward, Johnny would play with the kids while I got dinner.

And while this tradition has helped Johnny and me connect and stay in touch with each other, it has also shown our kids that our relationship as husband and wife is top priority.

— ❧ —

In a non-threatening way, we need to explain to our husbands why communication is so important to us. We must avoid berating our mates for not "opening up" and, instead, tell them of our desire to be more involved in their lives. When Johnny seems unusually quiet, I've said something like, "Honey, when you don't say anything to me when you're down, my imagination goes wild. I wonder what I've done, or if you're upset with me." That opens the door for him to talk about his emotions.

It seemed to me that every Saturday for years, Johnny was typically in a bad mood and I couldn't figure out why. I assumed I was somehow the "problem." Finally, I asked him why he was always so edgy on Saturday. He told me it was because he was preoccupied with his sermon for Sunday. It had nothing to do with me or the children. It had to do with the pressure he was under "to perform." Now he'll say, "Gang, I want you all to know right up-front that I think you're all wonderful. If I'm testy, it has nothing to do with you. I'm really stressed out because my sermon is not done."

You should also explain to your husband that you want him to feel free to talk to you about all areas of his life. For example, I think it's important for a husband to talk to his wife about his work. Tell him you want to better understand how he spends a major portion of his time. Tell him you're interested in every detail because you love him.

Also, express to him your willingness—your need—to share his work frustrations. Some men don't want to "burden" their wives with their work problems. But it is much worse for a man to come home one day and tell his wife he is in danger of losing his job without having shared with her any of the problems that led up to it.

Making Home a Haven

I've found that good communication occurs most freely in a home where the tension is minimal. Home needs to be a refuge—a place where we're safe, where we're encouraged and appreciated, where we have some peace. Peace doesn't mean quiet. With five children—nearly all teenagers—my home is Grand Central Station! Rather, quiet means amicable; the absence of hostility.

Second Corinthians 2:14-16 calls us to be the aroma of Christ in every place. And "in every place" certainly begins with the home. I want my home to radiate the fragrance of Christ. Practically speaking, my home should be a positive place. A place where each family member is built up.

How do we do this? Well, one thing I try to do consistently is meet my family at the door with a kiss and a smile when they come home from school or work. Many times I don't feel like doing it! But I do it anyway. I remember that we don't live life based on feelings, but based on conviction. If I waited until I felt like doing something, chances are I'd never do it.

Another thing I do is turn on the answering machine during dinner time. This gives us nearly an hour to share together as a family—without interruptions.

Because everybody's different, I think it's helpful for wives to find out how they can make their home a more comfortable, peaceful place for their husbands. For example, my friend Scott says he needs a relaxing atmosphere to open up. What he wants when he comes home from work is a chance to listen to some praise tapes and crash on the couch with his golden retriever. That transition time is important to him. After he's had that private time, he's ready to talk about his day and listen to his wife's concerns.

Find out what works best for you and your husband, then stick to it. As I said earlier, don't bank on your feelings, bank on conviction. And then reap the benefits: an enhanced opportunity for you to be a part of your husband's life, and for your husband to be more a part of yours.

———— ❦ ————

I've noticed that Johnny is more likely to openly communicate with me if I take time to affirm him. If your husband *knows* he's unconditionally accepted by you, then that sense of security will encourage him to share deeply.

For example, Johnny gets up around 5:30 every morning to have some quiet time before the family gets up. I've always been grateful to know he's downstairs praying for us. But I realized one morning that I had never told him how much that means to me. So one day I did. How often we appreciate things but fail to verbalize them.

We build up not only by affirming, but also by refusing to reject or criticize. None of us feels comfortable talking about something if we fear we will be rejected for what we say. If your husband opens up and he's not accepted or he's criticized, he'll likely withdraw into his shell.

Suppose a husband shares his idea for a dream trip to Europe. If the wife's reaction is, "Oh, yeah, sure. How are we going to accomplish that? We can't even pay the bills," he'll be more hesitant to tell her the next time he has a grand idea. If she shoots him down consistently, he'll stop sharing his dreams altogether.

Affirmation is something we need to do beginning the first day of our marriage and from every day forward. We need to remember we're married for life. It's a covenant relationship and it's forever. While at times it might be difficult, resist the temptation to berate those ideas and dreams your husband shares. Be thankful he is sharing and keep building him up because then he'll be more apt to share with you.

We can also show more sensitivity by asking good questions. Ask both information questions and feeling questions. An information question would be, "What happened at your lunch meeting?" Feeling questions would be more along the lines of, "How does this pressure make you feel?"

As I said earlier, men don't tend to think about their feelings as much as women. I remember when I first started asking Johnny about his feelings. He said, "I don't feel about things. I just do my work." But eventually he began to realize he did feel encouraged, angry, or frightened about things. Men do feel, but they often bury their feelings. A wife can help her husband get in touch with his emotions by gently probing him with questions.

Sometimes it threatens a man to ask him, "Tell me what's going on inside of you." When I say that to Johnny, he just groans. But if I ask him a specific question, he can answer it. For example, "Tell me about a good talk you had with somebody at the office today." Or, "Tell me something that happened at work today that made you feel good about yourself." Specific questions are much easier to handle than more general questions like, "How are you feeling?"

When you're asking your husband questions, tell yourself your goal is to understand him, not solve his problems. A friend of mine who's married to a rather withdrawn man, said that this has been the single most important lesson she's learned in bringing out her quiet husband. She has to fight the tendency, daily, to come up with resolutions.

If we always have a solution to "their" problem, we are in essence saying we are better problem-solvers than they are. Such a nonverbal message can effectively kill any husband's willing-ness to be vulnerable. Unless they ask us for advice, what they really need is someone to listen.

— ❧ —

Openness and vulnerability can be learned from someone modeling them. Your husband can learn from your example. If your husband is uncomfortable with being vulnerable, talk to him about things other than your marriage relationship. Tell him about your struggles at the office, or about a tough relation-ship with a neighbor. Talk about *your* feelings. Ask him what his insights are and ask him to pray for you.

Remember that acceptance and love will promote vulnera-bility. If we show and tell our appreciation for our husbands, if we "build each other up," then being vulnerable will be less threatening.

The Role of Friends

Your husband's friends can also help draw out his thoughts and feelings. I previously mentioned a retreat Johnny and I take with close friends every year. These weekends have taught me a lot about Johnny. At some point during the weekend each per-son takes a turn sharing the highs and lows of the past year. What has happened in my relationship with the Lord? How am I doing in my profession?

We also have friends locally with whom we get together. One man, Doug, is a wonderful questioner. He will say, "Johnny, what is happening in your life that you're excited about?" Or, "How do you feel about things on the job right now?" One's an information question and one's a feeling question. And often I learn things in the context of conversation with another couple that I didn't know about Johnny.

My encouragement to you would be to develop close rela-tionships with one or two other Christian couples, and build up a rapport so that you're getting to know each other as couples.

— ❧ —

My women friends also play an important role in developing good marriage communication. Women have a tremendous need for sharing and intimacy. And I've found that my friends keep me from relying on Johnny to meet all my emotional needs—something only God can do.

So it's vital to make time for friendships. If you work outside the home, use lunch hours to visit and deepen friendships on the job. Or if you're home with children, make regular dates at the park where the kids can play and you can talk. Young mothers especially need the emotional support of other women who can identify with what you're going through. The same can be said of mothers of adolescents, and women facing mid-life crisis.

Friendships do take time, and increasingly, that's a commodity in short supply. But I've learned again and again that the benefits of a nurtured friendship far outweigh the time invested.

———— ·⊱❧⊰· ————

Perhaps your husband isn't strongly communicative. Perhaps he's not your best friend. And yet, within the covenant of marriage, we have a lifetime in which to build a wonderful best friendship.

So don't be discouraged. As I said at the beginning of the chapter, building good communication skills takes time. The situation you find yourself in right now may be the very one God wants to use to mold you into the person he wants you to become. We can either resent the communications challenge—clam up and silently withdraw from our spouse—or we can see it as an opportunity for God's grace to flow through us and draw us more intimately together.

Must Men Be Emotional No-Shows?
Eileen Silva Kindig

Donald Bell sheds some light on the dilemma of communication between men and women in his book *Being a Man*. According to Bell, men and women have very different styles of communication. Women tend to communicate on three levels—topical, relational, and personal—while men generally confine themselves to the topical. To men, talking about what happened at work, whether or not the lawn needs aerating, and the progress of the kids' orthodontia is the stuff of which marriage is made.

Also, topical sharing is safe. For some men, venturing into the relational realm is risky. Discussing marriage, friendships, and family members will undoubtedly involve feelings. Talking about deeply personal things, even with the person you promised before God to love, honor, and cherish, can be profoundly scary when you've been conditioned to "be a soldier" and "never let 'em see you sweat." Defenses don't come tumbling down on demand. Times may have changed, but most men are finding it tough to shuck off three decades or more of conditioning overnight.

Yet, there is hope. Although most women consider themselves more empathetic than their mates, research has shot welcome holes through the theory. According to exhaustive studies at the University of Arizona, men equal women in understanding and compassion—it's just that men are not as comfortable showing it. Women with successful marriages understand this and gently lead their men down the path of open dialogue.

"Absolutely!" agrees my friend Jessica. After fifteen happy years in her second marriage, she feels she's been through the communication trenches. "Tom was no different than any other man when we married. But I treated him the way I wanted him to treat me and little by little he began to open up. I think too many women whine and demand intimacy. But it's not something you can order like a cheeseburger to go."

Family therapist Patricia Parr of Medina, Ohio, concurs. She also brings up another crucial point that's often overlooked by spouses who claim lack of communication.

"People can never *not* communicate," she insists. "Even silence communicates something."

Parr further emphasizes "meta-communication," or the unspoken message behind the words. If wives listen carefully, they can often pick up clues to their husband's emotions. Too often, women don't pay attention to the stories of what's happening at work or the fact that he wants to wait until next year to paint the house. Intimacy, they figure, isn't about what the boss said but instead about sunsets and dreams for the future.

I know from my own marriage that one of the most intimate conversations my husband and I ever shared was about redecorating our house. We had just moved into our home and my husband had become like a man possessed, replacing floor coverings, wallpaper, and counter tops. Every spare minute went into the process. For two months we argued until I finally realized that behind all the activity loomed my husband's loud message—"I feel overwhelmed here and can't rest until this is finished! Our home is important to me and I'm embarrassed by its present condition."

Once I realized this and put it into words for him, he was able to tell me his dreams for the place. This led to sharing about our childhood homes and how our house reflected who we are as people and as a couple. The battleground turned into a meeting ground.

From Today's Christian Woman
(March/April 1990)

Make It Happen

1. Determine with your spouse when there is a natural "talk time" during your day. For some, it is a post-dinner cup of coffee. For others, it's after the kids are in bed.

2. Think about the atmosphere you'd like to have characterize your home. Get your husband to do the same. Then discuss your ideas. Decide on one thing you can do to make your home more like the ideals you've both described and start there in moving your hopes toward reality.

3. Pay attention to the questions you hear on television interviews or in social settings. Find out what kinds of questions bring worthwhile answers. Notice the kinds of questions you ask people. Are they open-ended? Informational? Feeling oriented? Also focus on how others question you and note your emotional response. As you become more aware of how you're communicating and responding, your ability to ask questions will improve. It takes time!

Chapter 8

DO I NEED TO TELL MY HUSBAND EVERYTHING?
Gigi Graham Tchividjian

am a very honest person, and Stephan and I have a very close relationship. We share almost everything but common sense dictates there is a difference between being honest and talking too much. For example, when Stephan thinks I'm doing too much, I don't go into grueling detail describing every writing deadline or speaking assignment facing me in the coming month. If I did, he'd get upset because he's concerned about me. Am I trying to deceive him? Absolutely not! If he asks about my schedule, I'll gladly tell him.

Does Oneness Mean Openness?

The goal in marriage is complete openness. After God created man and woman, it says in Genesis, "The man and his wife were both naked, and they felt no shame." This refers to more than just physical nakedness. It refers to a nakedness of soul and spirit as well. Our greatest longing is to have someone with whom we can share everything; someone who will understand and accept us for who we are.

Not too surprisingly, then, there are those who feel husbands and wives should tell each other everything. Tell each other when you're angry or tell each other the little things the other does that are annoying. It seems most of this belief is based on the thinking that complete honesty will keep your marriage clear of misunderstanding and give you a closer, more open relationship. While this is true, wisdom, common sense, and a loving, compassionate spirit are needed as well. Complete honesty is ideal, but we are dealing with relationships that have been affected by the Fall. Each spouse is imperfect. It really helps if I can remind myself that I am married to an imperfect person and so is Stephan.

Over time, I've come to adhere to the view of openness that says you don't have to talk about every little detail of your life. Trust and respect for one another are very important. So if I felt that I had to check with Stephan on every detail, or "check in" each night, I would feel a lack of respect and trust. Stephan doesn't need to tell me where he ate lunch, with whom or how much he paid. Neither do I. We trust each other. But we enjoy sharing our days. And there are some things you simply put up with—without mentioning them.

When Stephan and I were first married, we talked about everything. But as we matured in our marriage, we learned the differences between what was important to talk about and what wasn't. For instance, when Stephan comes home from work, I try to judge how much to tell him about my day. If I detect he's had an especially hard day, I may not tell him all the bad things the children did or share all my frustrations. It's not that I'm hiding things from him, rather I'm protecting him. He doesn't need additional problems dumped in his lap the moment he walks through the door. When the time is right, I'll share my concerns.

However, there is one caution to keep in mind. As you decide what to tell your husband and what not to tell him, ask yourself, "Am I trying to hide something to protect myself?" Also, if you keep secrets from him it could mean you have let something in your life get out of control and you don't want to admit it.

For example, I have a few friends who go to great lengths to hide their spending sprees from their husbands. One friend bought too many clothes on a recent shopping trip, so she sent them to the cleaners before she wore them. Then when her husband said, "Isn't that a another new dress?" she could say, "No, I've already sent this to the cleaners." She was telling the truth about the cleaners, but essentially she was deceiving her husband to hide her out-of-control spending habits which could lead to deeper problems. So as we decide what to tell our husbands, we need to check our motives.

One area where I would encourage openness is in sharing your hopes and dreams. It might be a dream for the future, or your frustration over a dream that seems to be sidelined with the demands of a growing family. But take time to discuss your hopes and dreams—even if they sound impossible or silly. I know some women who feel a sense of regret because a certain dream wasn't fulfilled. Yet after talking with them, I realized one reason the dream died was because they never took time to share it with their husbands and work together on making the dream come true. You never know what can happen once you open up that "secret" side of yourself.

> ### The Good, the Bad, and the Funny
>
> We often wonder whether or not to tell our husbands about the bad things in our past. But let's not forget there's a lot in our past, in our family backgrounds, that isn't negative. Sharing those things can help our husbands know us better. Our past defines who we are. We should tell them all we know about our families, what we admire about our grandmothers, what we remember about kindergarten, and so on. All those things will bond a husband and wife closer to each other.
>
> —Susan

A Word about Past Indiscretions

Much of the discussion over the "how honest is too honest?" question in marriage concerns the confessing of past indiscretions. For example, let's say you were sexually active with another man before marrying your husband—a situation more and more men *and* women are finding themselves in. Should you tell your husband about this involvement? Is it even necessary?

Defeating Temptation

When I was about twelve years old, my mother felt an attraction to a very saintly minister in our denomination. Every time she heard him speak, she felt drawn to him. I don't think there was ever a word between them; they lived in different towns. But the attraction itself made her uncomfortable. She would find herself thinking about what an incredible person he was.

Finally, she sat my father down and said, "Lee, I want you to pray about something. I feel an attraction to this man. I've never had a word with him. Never a note written. But I feel I can't get victory over these feelings without your help."

And so my dad, cool as a cucumber, said, "Sure, let's pray about it." And then he prayed, and that was the end of it. Mother said the minute she admitted her thoughts and feelings to her husband and invited his prayer, the problem left.

I admit, not every man is as secure as my father. Some would be very threatened by that kind of disclosure. But if more people could turn to their spouse in similar situations, marriages would be a lot better.

—Gloria

While I encourage openness, I wouldn't advocate telling every detail of the indiscretion. Explicit details could paint pictures in your husband's mind that might be difficult for him to erase.

If you are going to disclose a past indiscretion, be willing to take some time to work through it. There will probably be repercussions. One woman I know admitted to her husabnd she had an intimate relationship with another man before their marriage. While they worked through the pain and reestablished trust in each other through counseling, they were separated for a year. They've been able to put their marriage back together again, but not without effort. It took them time to sort through the many emotions that surfaced after her confession.

Of course, one benefit of such a disclosure is the possibility of forgiveness. Knowing your husband has forgiven your past helps you to have the assurance that God has forgiven you. Otherwise, I think you might wonder, "If I don't know if my husband would forgive me for this, how do I know that God has forgiven me?"

If you decide not to tell your husband about your past, but still feel guilty, perhaps you need somebody to confide in, someone to advise you. You might want to seek out a mature Christian friend who will pray with you and assure you of God's forgiveness.

You can get assurance of forgiveness from Scripture alone, but I don't think Scripture teaches that we have to go it alone. That's where Christian friends come in, or perhaps your pastor. Galatians 6:2 reminds us, "Carry each other's burdens, and in this way you fulfill the law of Christ."

If you share your problem with a friend or pastor, and confess it to God in front of this person, you will be able to look back and say, "On such and such a date, I asked God to forgive me and I know he has." There is good reason so many of us were taught 1 John 1:9 as children. It's truth is basic and profound: "If we confess our sins, he is faithful and just and will forgive us our sins and purify us from all unrighteousness."

Once confessed, you've got to put your sin behind you and go on. That doesn't mean you'll never think of it again, but that you won't dwell on it. Instead, you can keep reminding yourself, "I've confessed this to God and he has forgiven me."

The Whole Truth?

Ephesians 4:15 tells us to speak the truth in love. That doesn't mean we have to say everything that comes to mind, even if it is "true." We have to exercise a little common sense and realize there are some things better left unsaid. Some things have no benefit to the other person. There have been times when I've thought about Johnny, "I don't like you at this moment." It's not going to be edifying to say that to him. Besides—I know these bad feelings are merely temporary. Some people feel they have to "spill their guts" about every little thing. I think that's a mistake.

—Susan

Openness: a Marriage Barometer

Reaching the level of openness God intends in our marriages comes down to developing a sense of unconditional love and acceptance in our marriages. It doesn't come automatically —it happens when we dare to be vulnerable and when that vulnerability is met with compassion.

Not long ago, I was reminded of the power of such unconditional acceptance and love. A woman had been sexually
abused as a child. For years, however, she suppressed those
memories. She married and raised a family. Then suddenly she
fell apart. Her husband didn't know what to do with her. He
finally brought her to see my husband. It took a lot of time and
many sessions to uncover the abuse in her past. When the truth
finally came out, her husband was overwhelmingly loving and
supportive. He could have been disgusted by her past or angry
for what she had put him through. Instead, his thought was,
"How can I help her get over this?"

As we develop our marriages, we increase the possibilities
of reaching the point where we can tell all and not fear the out-
come.

How Honest Is Too Honest?
Carole Mayhall

Can we be too open? Too transparent? Is there a
point where honesty ends and hurt begins?

To be "transparent," according to Webster, is to be
"without guile and concealment; open; frank; candid."
To many, that means being able to say anything that
pops into your mind without restraint. We are told
this approach fosters intimacy, so we yield to its
appeal until we discover it can destroy the very relationships we hold dear.

But why does transparency become destructive
at times? To begin with, *transparency isn't necessarily honest.*
My feelings and thoughts are extremely changeable.
My reactions many vary from month to month—
even hour to hour. I'm hard put to know which is the

real me. At that "time of the month" I can be short-tempered and feel absolutely worthless to myself and to the world. A week later, my responses may be totally different. To allow my husband to be the dumping ground for my mixed-up temporary feelings not only is inconsiderate, but also possibly dishonest. It will never lead to the intimacy I desire.

Transparency also can be the enemy of intimacy. Some time ago, a friend confessed she was jealous of a woman her husband had to work with for the summer. She knew her jealousy was unfounded, and her husband had no choice but to work with the other woman. But she wanted to be honest and let her husband know how she felt. "Should I tell my husband?" she asked. After we talked, she realized sharing her feelings would only make him more uncomfortable and actually more aware of the other woman. She decided it would be more kind and loving to wait and share her feeling *after* the summer had ended. Then, rather than strain the relationship, her openness would generate caring communication.

Finally, *transparency often is not kind.* Cleaning the barbecue grill is one of my most detested jobs. Yet one August before company arrived, I decided to clean it. In the middle of the job I went inside for more paper towels and saw my husband, Jack, who is trying hard to exercise regularly, resting with his feet up. "I walked five miles today," he said proudly.

Between clenched teeth, I replied, "Think what you could have accomplished with that energy."

I watched the joy of accomplishment drain from his face. I'd been transparent, all right—I'd said exactly what I'd been thinking but I was totally wrong to say it because it was unkind.

> If what we call transparency is really bluntness, if it is unkind and unloving, then we are disobeying Scripture, and honesty is not the best policy. According to the Bible, truth must be married to love; honesty must be intertwined with kindness.
>
> *From* Today's Christian Woman
> *(November/December 1989)*

Make It Happen

1. Ask yourself how you would respond if your husband told you he had sex before marriage. Your answer might indicate the strength of your relationship and help you decide whether or not to tell him about your past.

2. Are there "little" things you should confess to your husband? Did you spend money on something he would not approve of? Did you lie to get out of doing something for him? Admitting those things will help you develop a more open, honest relationship.

3. Think about some personal dreams you've set aside because of the demands of marriage or family. Tell your husband about them. He'll know you better for it, and may be able to help you find a way to make those dreams come true.

Chapter 9

HOW DO I HANDLE CONFLICT IN MY MARRIAGE?
Susan Alexander Yates

I n any marriage, and I emphasize *any*, fights happen. Irritations explode into anger. Words are said. Feelings are hurt.

I can still vividly recall the first big argument Johnny and I had shortly after we were married. I should say I remember the culmination of that fight. Johnny and I were heatedly disagreeing with each other. After a few minutes of arguing, I finally burst out in tears and said, "Maybe we just shouldn't have gotten married."

I'll never forget Johnny's reaction. His response took me completely by surprise. With a sense of fierce conviction that I'd never seen in him before he said, "Never, ever say such a thing again." I was so astounded by his response I didn't say another word. And believe me, I have never since questioned if we should be married.

Looking back, our first fight taught me several valuable principles about marital anger. First, it taught me that no one is immune. As basic as that statement may seem, it's common sense many Christians have a tough time dealing with. We usually interpret our anger as sin, which isn't always the case. As

Johnny puts it, if you don't experience anger occasionally, then you aren't taking life seriously enough. If you're a passionate person, you will get angry.

Second, that early fight taught me that anger can serve to put what's most important into perspective. Johnny's reaction to my "shouldn't have married me" speech underscored the covenant reality of our marriage. Our marriage is permanent—and statements questioning that permanence are clearly not allowed.

Of course, such principles rarely ease the pain of an explosive moment. Nor do they always assure us that anger won't grow into bitterness. For that reason, then, it is important to evaluate our anger and understand its sources so that we can work together to resolve its tensions.

Check Your Attitudes and Expectations

Whether we want to admit it or not, marriage brings together two self-centered people whose natural instincts are to please themselves. And it's this self-centeredness that is undoubtedly the premier cause of conflict. Yet, God has called us to a life of sacrifice, particularly in the framework of marriage. That's what makes the Christian marriage so radically different. Rather than asking myself, "how can I get Johnny to give me my way," I have to instead ask myself, "how can I create a house that isn't full of tension?"

For instance, we all have a tendency to nag when we're frustrated by something our spouse is—or isn't—doing. When these tension points arise, I could keep nagging or I could sit down with Johnny and brainstorm a solution.

Because we Yates' now have four drivers in the family, our two cars can be a real mess filled with school papers, dirty napkins, and empty soda cans. Johnny gets frustrated with me when I don't clean them up, and I get frustrated because whenever I'm leaving the car, my hands are usually full of groceries, the drycleaning, or a briefcase. I don't really feel Johnny's expectation is fair. To go back out and clean the car takes additional effort. But I need to remember my goal is to not please myself but instead ease those tension points.

At a brainstorming session, Johnny and I need to come up with a plan to alleviate this continual frustration. Maybe it means setting up a schedule for the kids to clean one car and for me to clean the other. But whatever we decide, our goal will be how to best prevent Johnny and me from nagging each other about keeping the cars clean.

Marriage requires a lot of compromise—and a lot of giving in to the other person. As married people we can no longer put ourselves first. We need to pray for a heart that wants to serve our mate. Ephesians 5:21 underscores this point, "Submit to one another out of reverence for Christ."

The Quick Fix

We live in an analgesic society. If it hurts, take an aspirin. If you don't like it, change it. If you don't want it, throw it away. We think we're not supposed to hurt. Well, yes, we are supposed to hurt. Hurt is part of life. It is part of growth. So if you come into a marriage thinking, "It's not supposed to hurt and if it starts to hurt, I'm out of here," you're less likely to work through problems. Divorce must never be perceived as an available alternative to conflict resolution.

—Gloria

———

One conflict resolving attitude I've tried to develop is that of giving my husband the benefit of the doubt—to believe the best. Of course, I hope he does likewise. We need to assume our husbands love us. Assume that just because he didn't have time to call today doesn't mean he's upset. Assume that just because he didn't tell us we look nice doesn't mean he thinks we're unattractive.

In other words, we need to grant one another grace. We live in such a perfectionist society that we don't allow one another the freedom to fail. For many years I was aggravated with Johnny when he didn't bring something home from the office I had specifically asked him for or didn't do something around the house. Finally it dawned on me that his forgetfulness wasn't intentional—he is just a very busy, involved man who works best if a request is in writing. Now I just write him notes!

Just as we women aren't always on top of our responses, so our husbands will have times of stress. Johnny doesn't think it's possible for any man to feel like he's on top of things at the office and on top of things with the family all at the same time. That's what women feel, too, and we forget men have those same kinds of frustrations. These tensions may interfere with your husband's ability to respond to you as he should.

Agree to Disagree

Many couples believe they have to agree on everything. The truth is, we only have to agree on the essentials, those things worthy of conviction. Our opposite traits are gifts God gives for the growing and molding of our relationships. Differences can be healthy. Sometimes we should agree to disagree. As my mother says, "If two people agree on everything, one of them is unnecessary."

—Gigi

Not every conflict will end in conciliatory hugs and kisses or simple solutions. Some problems will come up again and again. I've found that besides adjusting my attitudes, I have to adjust my expectations as well.

A recurring tension in my marriage is the rub between Johnny's work schedules and our time as a family. As a minister, Johnny has essentially a twenty-four-hour-a-day job. It's not uncommon for him to come home for dinner, relax for a hour, then head out to yet another meeting that lasts until 10:00 P.M. Invariably, once or twice a year we'll have a blowup. And, as the keeper of the family schedule, it's always me telling Johnny that "something has to give" on his work schedule. I need him and so do the children. And once again, the demands of the ministry are overtaking family time.

While my anger has helped us rethink our priorities, it has never resolved the tension to my satisfaction. And up until a few years ago, I was frustrated because there wasn't a solution. No matter how hard we worked at easing the tension, our solutions only seemed temporary. What I really wanted was something permanent.

Then God began to deal with me: "Susan, this is the cutting

edge in your marriage and it will *never* be solved. This is where you'll have to trust me and you'll have to continue to grow."

The problem would never be solved? Oddly, that realization gave me a real sense of peace. Because of the nature of Johnny's job and the fact that schedules always have some uncertainty, my trying to "fix" this problem was a waste of time. And once I accepted this, I took the first steps in lowering my expectations. I am beginning to be content with schedule "compromises" as opposed to schedule solutions. If Johnny can't make it to one of the kids' games, I try to accept the fact my expectations of a perfect family outing won't be realized this particular time.

Of course, the tension remains, but with God's grace, I'm learning to view it as a creative tension—one that forces Johnny and me periodically to make hard choices and always to seek God's guidance.

———— ❧ ————

It is also important to acknowledge the role of personality differences in igniting anger. We tend to think people see things our way and all approach a problem from the same point of view. Given my personality traits, I'm going to solve a problem in a certain way or react a certain way while my husband is going to respond another way.

Your differences can be either irritants or blessings. It depends on your perspective. For instance, my husband is even tempered. He's a rock, and initially that's what attracted me to him. I knew he would never do anything bizarre. But after a few years of marriage, I'll admit life became a little too predictable. I've caught myself wishing Johnny would do something terribly creative like plan a surprise party for my birthday or send me flowers for no reason. Yet doing something spontaneous and crazy is not his way to communicate affection. I came to the point where I said, "Okay, I have a choice. I can be irritated because he's not doing what I like; or I can be thankful because his rock solid nature gives me the freedom to be creative."

Problems will reveal personality differences. Yet these

differences are what make us better as a couple than we are as individuals. Consequently we must view problems as opportunities rather than opponents because they help us discover more about ourselves and our mates.

Practical "Resolution" Strategies

Not long ago, a friend was telling me how she had successfully handled her anger. It seems she was seething over what she thought was a very rude comment her husband made to a house guest. Fortunately, she kept her angry feelings intact and didn't say anything until the company had left. "I really wanted to let my husband know how angry I was right then," she admitted, "but I made myself go to the bedroom for twenty minutes and collect my thoughts."

Later she returned to the family room and found her husband watching television. "I asked him if he was engrossed in the show, and when he said no, I asked if we could turn the TV off for a minute and talk," she said.

"Since I had time to cool off, I was able to calmly tell my husband what I observed and how it made me feel," she continued. "In fact, I asked if I was interpreting the events right. Then he explained his view of the situation and why he reacted as he did. Believe it or not, we were both able to vent our feelings and it didn't end in a yelling match."

My friend's story brings up some excellent ways to communicate better and resolve conflict. Despite her anger, she showed respect for her husband by not arguing in front of others —something "the others" I'm sure appreciated. Next she waited so she wasn't tempted to act out of anger and gave herself time to think about what she wanted to say before she confronted her husband. Then she picked a good time to talk over her feelings and did so without accusations.

All of these steps led to a calm discussion of a tense situation. And although my friend admitted she wasn't completely satisfied with her husband's explanation of his behavior, at least he knew how she felt and she was no longer angry.

I can't emphasize enough how important it is to pick an appropriate time to discuss an unresolved issue. It took me several years to realize timing can be everything when it comes to resolving a conflict. For instance, I've learned not to bring up a heavy issue right after Johnny gets home from Sunday services. Also, Johnny and I try not to talk when we're tired. Neither one of us does very well late at night.

Of course, with a busy family life and my husband's demanding job, the right times may not always present themselves. So one thing I've done on occasion is to make an appointment with Johnny to discuss a problem which needs to be solved. While it sounds formal, it does work. Besides making us set aside a time to talk, it also gives us time to think about the problem.

Johnny and I try not to go to bed angry with each other. Even if we can't resolve an issue—and even if we don't feel like it—we offer each other forgiveness and promise that we'll continue to work out the problem. This isn't the same as denying our problems and pretending everything is "hunky dory." It simply forces us to affirm our love for each other and diffuse the anger that may be building up between us. The hurt may well remain. But because we live under covenant, we need to be united.

When you do find a good time to talk about something that is making you angry, choose your words with care. What we want to do is attack problems, not people. A familiar, useful suggestion is to express your concerns using "I" statements, clarifying how you feel. "I was bothered when you . . ." sets a much better tone than saying, "Johnny, you were so rude." Comments like the latter attack the core of a person, making him or her defensive and unable to respond calmly.

One good way I've found to guard my words is to put them in writing. I actually write letters to my husband. Writing helps me organize my thoughts. Also, if I write something down about how I'm feeling, I have the option to scratch it out. Usually I wait twenty-four hours before giving a letter to my husband—time enough for me to *really* think through what I said. And when I hand over the letter, I always say, "Think about what I've said. I hope we can talk it over."

Avoiding Conflict When Possible

It's best, of course, if conflicts can be avoided. And one way to do this is to anticipate problems. Vacations and holidays can become fertile grounds for conflict. We get ourselves in many muddles because we haven't thought ahead. And then we respond with emotion to a crisis. Johnny and I now sit down in the fall and think through our options for the holidays. Once we agree on what is best for our immediate family, then we can respond to requests from extended family and friends.

September is always an exceptionally busy month. Everything starts up. School starts and there are lots of "back-to-school" meetings for parents. The years' ministry at the church gets underway with several "kick-off" events. Teams and clubs recruit the kids, and it's easy to find one's family simply passing in the driveway. Meaningful communication can dwindle between mates. And tempers are likely to flare as both parents cope with the pressures of a hectic schedule

One year, after a particularly difficult September, Johnny and I determined that the next fall we would devise some "protection plan" before September began. We decided to carefully consider the activities that our children should be involved in. And we agreed to put on the calendar times to be together as husband and wife, and as a family during this difficult "start-up" month.

When we go through times of conflict in our marriage, it is important to ask ourselves two questions:

What have we learned from this situation?

What positive steps can we take to avoid similar conflicts in the future?

Another way to anticipate potential conflict is to find out as much as you can about each other's backgrounds. Watch each

other in as many different family situations as you can. You'll undoubtedly see some irritants that have infected your own marriage by way of his, or your, family.

A friend of mine is married to a truly likable man. Yet he is also rather quiet and isn't very comfortable sharing his feelings. More than once my friend has expressed her frustration and anger about her stoic husband. "Just once I wish he'd tell me how he's feeling without me having to pry it out of him," she said.

For her a light went on when she started to study her husband's family. She began to notice how quiet her father-in-law was and how his quietness had resulted in her husband having very little emotional attachment to his father. Soon she realized that because of her husband's upbringing he simply didn't know how to express his feelings.

Over time my friend changed her approach. Rather than complain about her silent husband or hope he'd change, she working at developing patience and understanding.

Whatever the severity of the conflict in your marriage, it needs to be discussed. It deserves to be worked on. How much better to resolve many small problems than to allow them to accumulate into a massive explosion. As one author said, "Keep short accounts."

"Lord, Help Rick Throw His Socks in the Hamper"
Bonnie Budzowski

Soon after I married, I realized I needed to pray daily for my marriage. But it was easy to catch myself muttering, "Lord, help Rick throw his socks in the hamper."

I needed simple prayers based on biblical

principles I could remember and use on the busiest of days. So I started praying, "Lord, help us to learn to cherish each other," every day. When I started using short sentence prayers, I noticed a real difference in my marriage. Whether my prayers grow out of what Scripture teaches about marriage, such as "Lord, help us to serve each other and you," or they spring from issues or problems I'm confronting, they deepen my marriage and make it more spiritually fulfilling. Here are some principles to help you formulate your own individual prayers.

Draw your prayers from Scripture. "Lord, help us to forgive each other freely" is important because we all fall short in marriage. Praying biblically gives you confidence that God will honor your prayers and shape your expectations for marriage in alignment with his Word.

Develop prayers that ask God to transform you and your husband into the image of Christ. I prayed, "Lord, let us treasure the things you treasure." Since prayers like this are not about things you want or consume, they will have lasting value.

Make sure your prayers are not complaints. Pray, "Lord, help us build up rather than tear down with our words," rather than, "Make my husband as good as I am at encouraging."

Make sure your prayers are practical. If they are simple rather than cumbersome or unfocused, you can find time and energy to use them daily. If they are from the heart, you will be motivated to use them. If you try a prayer and find that for some reason you are not comfortable with it, change the prayer.

These short, simple prayers have eased the tension between my goal of praying consistently for my marriage and the rush of daily duties. Sentence prayers cannot take away the need for prayer for and with our husbands. But single sentences, uttered faithfully and sincerely before God, can have a genuine impact on our marriages. What will your sentences be?

From Today's Christian Woman
(January/February 1991)

Make It Happen

1. Write yourself a contract that pinpoints one area of conflict resolution you need to work on and determine to make a change. For instance, your contract might read, "I hereby resolve never to bring up a problem when we're both tired." Date it and sign it. When you've got one area under control, move on to something else.

2. Investigate some personality profiles. Take one yourself and see if your husband would be willing to take one too. One popular test is the Myers-Briggs profile. Check your local library or contact the publisher for the book Myers-Briggs Type Indicator by Isabel Briggs Myers and Katherine C. Briggs, Consulting Psychologists Press, Inc., Palo Alto, California 94306.

3. What problems can you anticipate in the next few months? Talk over holidays, changes in schedule—whatever might be a potential conflict. Develop strategies you and your husband can use to handle these potential conflicts more constructively once they arrive.

Chapter 10

WHEN IS FORGIVENESS NEEDED IN MARRIAGE?
Gigi Graham Tchividjian

When is forgiveness needed? Daily. The late Robert Quillan once described marriage as "the union of two good forgivers." As I understand it, there are two areas where forgiveness is needed in marriage. First, there are the daily irritations and annoyances that we all experience in marriage. Some of these simply need to be overlooked. Others need to be addressed and discussed so that these small irritations and offenses won't build into resentfulness and bitterness. And it's often the daily forgiveness of those minor irritations most of us can readily identify with.

For instance, not long ago, I was preparing to leave to go speak at a nearby conference. I asked Stephan if he would load several boxes of books into the trunk of my car as I have a bad back and lifting heavy boxes might mean spending the next week in bed.

"I'll do it in a few minutes, honey," he replied, intently watching the evening news.

Stephan tends to be forgetful, so it wasn't surprising that after the news was over, he forgot my request.

So I asked him again. Yet by bedtime, the books were still not in the car.

"Honey," I said, "Let's go out and put those boxes in the car. It settles my mind to know they're in the car."

"I told you," Stephan said a bit impatiently, "I'll do it. Those boxes *will* be in your car before you leave tomorrow morning."

I decided not to say another word. Yet the next morning, the boxes were still in the hallway and Stephan was already at work. I lifted them into the trunk, bad back and all, and went off to my conference—frustrated and hurt.

A few days later, Stephan came to me and apologized. "Gigi," he said, "I was sitting in the middle of a counseling session when it suddenly dawned on me that I'd forgotten to put those books in your car. I'm really sorry!"

Forgetfulness, misunderstandings, and a thousand other irritants have a way of cutting at a marriage. But how we treat those everyday annoyances can mean the difference between temporary unpleasantness and long-term hurt.

I accepted Stephan's apology. After twenty-eight years of marriage I know he didn't mean to hurt me, and I also know that not accepting his apology could have resulted in additional anger, hurt feelings, and bitterness—not exactly the ingredients of a happy marriage. After all, Proverbs 10:12 tells us, "Hatred stirs up dissension, but love covers over all wrongs." In other words, love chooses to forget.

—⋘⋙—

Many of the mosquitoes in a marriage can be swatted away by fostering a "get over it" attitude. Take the box episode I just described. Sure I was angry and frustrated. Stephan should have done what I asked. And I could have let my irritation over the incident brew, but I made myself stop and listen to common sense—are forgotten boxes really worth a major marital dissension?

I'm convinced that one of Satan's tricks is to close our minds to common sense. When that happens, we soon find ourselves consumed by minor offenses. And I know how easily that can happen. The entire way to the airport that day, all I could think about was, "Why couldn't Stephan have helped me with my simple request? Why does he have to be so forgetful? If he really loves me he would have loaded those boxes."

Instead of thinking about the women I would be ministering to I was indulging in a "pity party." I was brooding over something of only momentary importance, which over time would be of little importance. As hard as it might seem at the moment, we have to make a conscious decision to let go. I needed to simply accept Stephan's apology, and say to myself, "These things happen. That's life." And then let go.

Someone once said that being a good parent is learning when to choose to ignore things. The same can be said about a good marriage partner. Move beyond those daily, minor irritations by simply choosing to ignore or at least choosing not to concentrate on the small infractions and then zero in on the positive aspects. I once heard Robert Schuller say, "Eliminate the negatives by accentuating the positives." How true this is in a loving marriage.

Making a Wrong, Right

One principle that is absolutely essential to feeling truly forgiven is restitution. If we have wronged another person, we must "make it right." Restitution hastens our healing.

Restitution might involve making a public apology. It could be repaying stolen money. Restitution could be painful, and it will probably cost us something. But there is nothing so valuable as going to bed at night knowing our conscience is clear before the Lord. It's a biblical principle and it's also psychologically sound. We must rid ourselves of guilt. It doesn't matter what it costs or how embarrassing it is—it's worth it to be clear before the Lord.

—Gloria

The What and When of Forgiveness

Of course, this doesn't mean little irritations should not be addressed. Every marriage experiences times when a husband or a wife goes through weeks—maybe months—where everything about the other person bothers them.

However, when these little irritations begin to multiply, we need to be on the lookout for signs of bitterness building up in our relationship. When this happens, just "getting over it" is not enough. We may need to discuss it in order to better understand each other.

Don't Just Say, "I'm Sorry"

When we have sinned against another, it's not enough to say, "I'm sorry." Those two little words don't demand a response. But when you say, "Will you forgive me?" you're asking for a response—a yes or no.

I don't ask forgiveness out of feeling, because I don't feel like doing it. I ask out of conviction. Johnny may not feel like forgiving me, but he does. And once we've settled that business, then God can heal the feelings.

—Susan

For instance, if Stephan's forgetfulness became an ongoing nuisance, I owe it to our relationship to bring it to his attention. Perhaps I need to take him out to dinner and say, "Honey, I need to talk to you. In the past four weeks, I have nicely asked you to do several things. Yet you always seem to forget and I'm a little hurt. I feel like you're always putting others first."

This will give us the opportunity to openly discuss what bothers us and try to find the cause of the irritant. It will also help us begin to correct it. Openly discussing small irritants is so much better than stuffing them further inside until frustration builds into a blowup.

— ❧ —

The second area where forgiveness is needed is when a serious wrong, like physical abuse or adultery, has occurred in a marriage. Sadly, I think many of us have been taught a lop-sided view of forgiveness. We constantly hear about the importance of unconditional forgiveness, yet what gets overlooked is repentance. God does not forgive us until we ask him to forgive. He stands ready to forgive—his arms are open wide. But that circle of forgiveness cannot be complete until we ask him to forgive us. If a woman's husband has been unfaithful, she can be ready and willing to forgive him, but if he has never asked for forgiveness, the circle is not complete.

Also, in some circumstances, there can be real and complete forgiveness without reconciliation. Again, we are living in an imperfect world with imperfect people affected by the Fall.

Consequently, some marriages have been broken and cannot be repaired although forgiveness has taken place.

No matter if we're talking about forgiveness of a myriad of "nuisances" or a major wrong in our marriage, we need to understand that forgiveness can't be based on feelings. Our feelings change. Forgiveness, however, is an act of obedience. An act of faith.

For instance, I don't *feel* converted a lot of the times. I have times of doubt. I ask questions like, "How in the world could God love me?" or " How could my acceptance of Christ when I was four-years-old be for good?" I look at all the things I've done between the time I accepted the Lord and today and I don't *feel* saved. But I am. Feelings are often Satan's contention for faith.

It's the same with forgiveness. Satan will come along and say, "You didn't really forgive that person. Remember all those terrible feelings you had when you thought about that person today?" But if we have forgiven, we can't rely on feelings.

One way I measure my forgiveness is by gauging my bitterness level. If I feel a sense of bitterness, then I know I've not truly forgiven. While often we still feel pain or sadness after we've offered forgiveness, bitterness has to go. It is something that gnaws at you, something that can grow to where it consumes you and can destroy any relationship, especially a marriage.

I have a friend who went through a divorce a number of years ago. I received a letter from her recently and could sense she was consumed by bitterness—over her divorce, over the settlement, over the fact that her ex-husband is remarried and has a child. She's engulfed by it. She may see her ex-husband in the mall one day and it may stir up all kinds of emotions. That's okay, that's normal. But forgiveness is living free of *consuming* bitterness.

Not allowing bitterness to take hold requires hard work. I know a couple who have made their marriage work, despite the husband's extra-marital affair. The wife chose to stay in the marriage because she remembered how wonderful it was before. It was something she wanted back. But I know for her the cost of forgiveness is a day-to-day thing—it means making a real effort not to remember, not to grieve over what happened, but to move on.

Forgiveness and Reconciliation

One misconception surrounding forgiveness is that once given, everything ends "happily-ever-after." Not so. Forgiveness does not eradicate the consequences of our sin. Rather, it provides two people the means to deal with those consequences.

God Can't Forgive That

If we can't forgive another person, we're implying that Christ's sacrifice wasn't sufficient. We're saying Jesus' dying on the Cross wasn't good enough.

If I'm not forgiving, then that's going to block what God can do with my life. More important than my marriage is my walk with the Lord. If I'm going to walk with the Lord, then I have to forgive.

—Susan

In another marriage I know of the husband is very repentant for his nearly five years of infidelity. And the wife has forgiven her husband for this serious breach in their marriage. But the foundations of the relationship were so damaged it simply couldn't be repaired and eventually they divorced. There was no story book ending here, but because of forgiveness, the couple are not absorbed in bitterness over the situation. Yet they still had to live with the sad consequences of sin—a broken marriage.

Forgiveness in Action

Remember, a good marriage is made up of two good forgivers. Forgiveness starts with a humble heart. This doesn't mean simply accepting every wrong done to us, or avoiding any loving confrontation of a wrong done too many times. Rather it means understanding that we, like our husbands, have been forgiven much. And with that perspective it puts us both on an equal footing.

Added to the humble heart we bring to our marriage should be our own commitment to the marriage. I'm married to Stephan for a lifetime. With this perspective, it's to our benefit to do what we can to keep our relationship running smooth and growing in love, not bitterness and resentment. Forgiveness makes that possible.

I don't think I've seen a better demonstration of how commitment and forgiveness work together than in one of my friend's situations. Through a series of unforeseen circumstances, her husband lost their entire savings, as well as a sizable personal trust fund from her grandparents. In fact, they lost more than their savings—they lost their house as well.

I once asked her, "How did you keep bitterness out of your marriage? You were a wealthy woman. Now you're going back to school so you can get a job to help support the family."

Her response was simple, but memorable. "For one thing, I don't languish over this mistake," she said, "But the main reason is commitment. I was committed to this man when I married him. I'm committed to him now—through thick and *thin*. The investment was a mistake. But I still love him." And, as she discovered, love is also a part of the commitment, not a feeling.

One of my favorite verses on marriage is Ephesians 4:32: "Be kind and compassionate to one another, forgiving each other, just as in Christ God forgave you."

Make It Happen

1. If you need to pray about a change in your attitude, write the prayer down. That will help you be more consistent and careful in your praying. Incorporate Scripture such as Matthew 6:14-15; 2 Corinthians 2:7-8; Colossians 3:13; Ephesians 4:32.

2. Make a list of your husband's positive traits. Remind yourself of them when you get frustrated with his weaknesses.

3. Write down the offenses about which you are bitter. Pray about them and then burn the list. When you're tempted to stew about one of the wrongs, remind yourself that it's nothing

but ashes and not worth ruining your health and relationship.

4. If you're having trouble forgiving your husband, tell a trusted friend or minister. Confessing your struggle will help you deal with it. That friend can also pray for you as you reach resolution.

Chapter 11

WHEN IS IT TIME TO SEEK PROFESSIONAL COUNSELING?

Gigi Graham Tchividjian

ears ago, when a woman encountered rough spots in her marriage, she would most likely seek out her mother or an older, experienced family member for a little advice. And usually, along with the advice would come the comforting words, "Honey, I faced much the same thing."

But today, extended family isn't always available. To take up the slack we have other "counselors," most often close, trusted friends or a tightly knit group at church. Yet even supportive friendships and church contacts seem to be vulnerable in our fast-paced, constantly changing world. Friends are suddenly transferred thousands of miles away and churches have grown to mega-churches that offer less opportunity to form intimate contacts.

So when problems arise in a marriage, the traditional "counselors" we once looked to for guidance aren't always available. And sometimes, even if you have family or friends to help—professional counseling is needed.

Breaking Down Misconceptions

Many people struggle with the appropriateness of counseling. Some view it as an outright confession of emotional instability. Still others, notably Christians, view professional counseling as a sign of spiritual weakness—a confession that you're out of step with God. They believe that the Lord and the Scriptures are enough to handle all of the problems that confront us.

Happily, I'm part of that pivotal generation where both viewpoints are being challenged. The truth is, there's no conflict between seeing a counselor or psychologist and Scripture. After all, Moses had his seventy counselors (Exodus 18). And the apostle Paul exhorted the church in Corinth not to be ignorant of his problems. Why? So that the church could help him physically, emotionally, and spiritually.

Stephan, like other Christians in the counseling profession, projects the Lord Jesus' compassion to hurting people. When you're in pain you don't need a three-point sermon, nor do you need to be yelled at or filled with guilt. What you need is someone to help you in solving your problem, and focusing on the hope in Christ. And that is where a Christian counselor can help a couple clearly see the principles taught in Scripture.

Going to a counselor is like getting another opinion on your situation. He is someone to help you think logically. When you're in the midst of a problem, things can be very muddled. You can't think objectively. But a good counselor can help you see through the fog. He is not someone who will tell you what to do, but rather help you develop insights into how to handle the situation from a biblical perspective.

For many problems, a session or two may be enough. For instance, my husband is a very insightful person, and after an hour or two with a couple he may be able to say, "This is the real problem, this is where you need to focus." Of course, there are cases where many sessions are needed in order to get to the source of the more complex problems in certain marriages.

The When of Counseling

Not every problem or rough time in a marriage means you need counseling. We all have times when our feelings for our husband wax and wane and the multiple obligations on us make the single life momentarily attractive. Such feelings are normal and need not make you wonder, "Should I get counseling?"

However, if you're beginning to feel that you are losing communication with your husband, or your lives are going in separate directions, and nothing you've done or your husband has done seems to be helping, then counseling is most probably needed.

People come for marriage counseling for many reasons. Many of the cases my husband sees could be described as guidance sessions—couples in need of some biblical common sense. In

Wanted: A Close Christian Friend

In some circles, going to a counselor has become the "in" thing to do. I'm reminded of the movie Crocodile Dundee, *where the backwoods Australian, Crocodile, comes to New York City. At a party, he overhears people talking about going to their "shrink," and asks a friend to explain. She tells him a shrink is a therapist, someone to tell your troubles to. To which Crocodile responds: "Don't these people have any mates?" meaning friends. There is definitely a need for professional counselors. But sometimes what is really needed is a close Christian friend.*

—Susan

these sessions, Stephan takes biblical principles and applies them to the client's situation, helping the client discover God's directives in a certain situation.

Others come to talk about communication breakdowns or moral problems like infidelity—situations that unfortunately are becoming more and more common.

I have a friend who was in business with her husband—a very successful business. Bit by bit they began to throw all of their energy into the business. Eventually, the husband had an affair. Thankfully my friend went into counseling as soon as she found out and over time so did her husband. It took months of counseling sessions, but the reason for the affair was finally uncovered.

It wasn't a lack of love or respect on the husband's part that lead to his unfaithfulness, instead it all came down to communication. One remark he made was, "At the end of the day I came home to a business partner. There was no one to talk to."

In my friend's case, the breakdown in communication led to a very serious problem in this marriage. But my friend and her husband learned many new communication skills, and their marriage survived intact.

Why Not Talk to a Stranger?

As you consider going to your pastor or church counselor, keep in mind that some husbands won't speak openly with somebody they know well. Your husband may not be comfortable admitting his problems to someone he plays basketball with on the church team. You can't get anywhere if you don't admit you have a problem, and sometimes people feel much more comfortable talking to an unknown third person.

—Gloria

One of the biggest problems with counseling is that people wait too long to seek help. Behavior patterns are so well established by the time people come in that it's often too late to rescue the marriage. This tendency to wait too long is especially common among Christians. One reason for this is that often the Christian tries to deal with problems on her own for so long that by the time she gets to a counselor she's moved beyond simple relationship problems into guilt and depression. A Christian woman becomes more and more guilty because now her spirituality is at stake. "I couldn't handle it on my own so what kind of Christian am I?" she thinks. "Can't the Lord deal with me? Why do I need to see a counselor?" Recently, I heard a Christian counselor say that so many Christians are dysfunctional because they are more concerned about maintaining an image than solving a problem.

Fortunately, there seems to be a greater acceptance of counseling and a greater willingness to seek out professional help when problems arise. This change in attitude is based on the realization that there are some problems just too big and too complicated for us to handle alone. And the Lord never meant for us to go it alone.

What If Your Husband Won't Go?

Often when a woman decides counseling would be a good option, her husband balks at the idea and simply refuses to go. Of course, it's preferable if both go, but counseling can still be beneficial if a woman goes alone. After all, the only person you can change is yourself. When we get to know ourselves better then we can know better how to react to certain circumstances.

If this is the situation you're facing, realize that your desire for counseling will show your husband you care about the relationship. Tell him saving your marriage is your motivation for going. Say something like, "I know you're uncomfortable with going to a counselor right now, but I'm concerned about our marriage. I'm going to see if I can find some answers. Or at least raise some good questions."

When Is a Counselor *Not* Necessary?
Louis McBurney

Before you reach for the Yellow Pages to call a marriage counselor, consider a couple of points. The first is that most marriages go through phases of closeness and distancing. These rhythms may last several months and are at the mercy of outside stresses, such as illness, demands from aging parents, problems with your children, career pressures, or major financial problems.

Certain life stages may also pull couples apart. For instance, childbirth, deaths of family members or friends, mid-life transition, the emptying of the nest, and menopause all tend to draw energy away from the marriage relationship. If you're at one of these stages, talk with your spouse about your concerns. It's possible that you may need patience more than psychology.

If you both desire to improve your marriage, consider alternatives to therapy. Marriage-enrichment seminars can work wonders to help you learn better skills in communication, conflict resolution, mutual understanding, and sexuality. Even reading a good book on marriage together may be the turning point you need.

From Louis McBurney, "Do You Need Counseling," Marriage Partnership magazine, Spring 1990. Used with permission.

Should My Counselor Be a Christian?

If you're looking for a counselor, I think a Christian counselor is preferable. Not simply because he is a Christian, but because the two of you together can draw from the Bible and bring its principles to bear on your particular situation.

Non-Christian counselors, while certainly capable of offering critical insights, cannot, as a rule, understand—or accept—our perspective on things. Their concept of guilt, for example, would be very different from ours. In fact, I've heard of some non-Christian counselors who have advised couples to go ahead and have an affair—all in an effort to revitalize a boring marriage. Needless to say, from a Christian point of view, such a method of revitalization is hardly the answer to anything.

Gigi Graham Tchividjian

Who Are the People Helpers?
Kelsey D. Menehan

People helpers go by many names and offer a wide range of abilities. Following are descriptions of some of them and what to look for.

Biblical counselor. The term may broadly refer to Christians who counsel, but usually it describes those who view the Scriptures as the *only* source of truth and use the Bible to confront a counselee with the need to change his attitudes or actions. Sometimes called "nouthetic counselors," these helpers may be self-taught or have completed a training program. Some proponents of this school of counseling believe that the pastor is the only one competent to counsel; others feel free to train lay Christians.

Marriage and family therapist. A counselor who focuses on dealing with problems within the family unit, he may have an educational background ranging from a bachelor's degree with some postgraduate training to a doctorate or medical degree. Look for membership in the American Association for Marriage and Family Therapy, at least a master's degree, and graduation from special family therapy courses.

Pastor. Many pastors have considerable experience and training in dealing with troubled people; but some do not. Especially if your problems are serious, don't be afraid to ask your pastor if he has received training in counseling. Does he recognize the validity of insights from psychology? Is he open to making referrals if your problems seem beyond his ability to help? If you are not satisfied with your pastor's answers, go elsewhere.

Pastoral counselor. A clergy or lay person who provides

private therapy, this helper may hold graduate degrees in psychology, social work, or family therapy. Look for certification from the American Association of Pastoral Counselors, plus a local license or other professional affiliation.

Psychiatrist. A medical doctor specializing in treating mental disorders, he is the only mental health professional who can prescribe drugs. A psychiatrist should have completed a residency in psychiatry, be board certified in psychiatry, and possess a license to practice medicine.

Psychoanalyst. Usually a psychiatrist, psychologist, or social worker who has undergone psychoanalysis before being allowed to use the treatment process on patients, he should be a graduate of an accredited psychoanalytic training institute.

Psychologist. He has earned a Ph.D. in either clinical or counseling psychology or psychoanalysis. Look for a diploma with the American Board of Professional Psychology, given to those who have been in private practice for more than five years. Other credentials are membership in the American Psychological Association, state or local license, and certification in a psychology specialty.

Social worker. This person frequently works in hospitals or community centers and helps people with special medical or psychological problems get the care they need. Some social workers have private practices. Look for certification by the Academy of Certified Social Workers, given to those who pass a written exam and have two years supervised experience and membership in the National Association of Social Workers.

From Today's Christian Woman
(May/June 1986)

Make It Happen

1. Take a risk and tell a few people at church you're considering counseling. You may be embarrassed at first, but you'll probably discover many of them have gone for counseling themselves and may be able to recommend someone to you.

2. If you feel a need for counseling but are reluctant, open up to a friend. She may be able to help you discover why you're hesitant. Are you afraid of ruining your "good" reputation? Are you afraid of confronting what's going on inside of you? Are you concerned about the cost? Whatever your hesitations, are they important enough to keep you from getting help?

3. Get involved in a "support" group. This may be as close as your Sunday school class or a young mother's group at church. Even if it isn't billed as a support group, you will find strength in associating with women who face the same things you do. And as you're open about your problems, you will probably find many kindred spirits.

MARRIAGE SPIRITUALITY

"A cord of three strands is not quickly broken"
(Ecclesiastes 4:12b).

hile there is, of course, no spiritual merit earned by being married, marriage nevertheless provides one man and one woman a unique spiritual testing ground—a soul-to-soul context for seeing if love, joy, peace, patience, kindness, goodness, faithfulness, gentleness, and self-control really do earmark the Christian couple committed to each other "for better or for worse, till death do us part."

Marriage can offer us a glimpse into our spiritual selves. It can expose both our strengths and our weaknesses, and it can give us a soul mate to whom we can bring both for mutual discussion, challenge, and prayer. Marriage has the potential of tightening our individual relational strand with God; and in so doing, draw us closer to our husbands as well.

In the following chapters, Gloria and pastor's wife Susan talk about the "how-tos" of nurturing individual faith both in Christian marriage and in marriages where the husband is not a believer.

Chapter 12

WHAT DOES SUBMISSION REALLY MEAN?

Gloria Gaither

 n America, at the end of the twentieth century, no one wants to think about—let alone live out—the much maligned command to "submit one to another" (Ephesians 5:21). Especially women. After all, why should we deny our recent social and cultural achievements by turning back the hands of time to a totally male-dominated age?

But submission—biblical submission—is anything but a clarion call for gender discrimination. Rather, when properly understood, it is a revolutionary formula for transforming husbands and wives into men and women of God.

———❦———

Ephesians 5:21 sets forth God's commission for anyone who names his name: "Submit to *one another* out of reverence for Christ." The word used for submit here means "under mission to." Thus, we are all called to be most intensely "under mission to" the primary relationships of our lives—beginning with our husbands. We are called to help them become all God wants them to be.

That means one day Gloria Gaither will stand and give an

account to God of whether or not she delivered unto the Kingdom the soul of Bill Gaither in its completeness, as gifted by God from the beginning, insofar as she was able. And Bill will one day stand accountable before God and give an account of the soul of Gloria and the completeness of her talents and abilities as God has gifted her. Likewise, we will both give an account of our children and our business relationships—and confess when selfish ambition or personal aspirations came in the way of our calling.

Submission will not afford us the "luxury" of blaming a spouse's authority for our own weaknesses. Rather, it places responsibility on each of us today to encourage our spouses, to be honest with them when we hurt, and to be confrontive when necessary, all in our efforts to fulfill our biblical mandate.

The paradox of "under mission to" submission when practiced in Christian marriage is that the "giver" also becomes a "taker." This has perhaps been no more apparent in my marriage than in Bill's decision to include me in what is now the Bill Gaither Trio.

Notice I said Bill's decision. I had absolutely no intentions of becoming a singer. In fact, I'm not a singer. (I only have a five note range!) But over twenty-five years ago, Bill recognized that when I communicated with people, something happened. So, he reasoned, if I just sang harmony, prayed, and told stories of God's working in our lives, God could use our music.

To say Bill's suggestion went down hard is an understatement. It precipitated the biggest spiritual struggle of my life. I argued with God, asking him to let me do the things I do well, like write and speak. And my pride was hurt; after all, I thought, not only don't I sing well, but audiences across the country will think I'm stupid for thinking I sing well!

But the humor of God! We had to start creating material that I could sing with my five-note range—and that's exactly what God had in mind. My weakness was forcing us to write songs that took theological concepts into everyday places. If I could sing these songs, anybody could sing them! We would never have been smart enough to say, "Let's create this wonderful, simple, new music form in which we take grand theological concepts and put them into singable songs so regular people with regular voices can sing them in regular places."

Today, I don't sing any better than I ever did. And frankly it's no easier. Every time Bill talks about a new album or the next tour, I get a huge knot in my stomach and want to run away. But I'm learning, with Bill's persistence, that God is bound to be exalted through my weakness. And somewhere in that weakness, I begin to better understand what he gifted me to do in the first place.

Like marital intimacy, mutual submission in marriage is an everyday matter. It's a process where each of you is challenging the other to do a new thing in faith, or to wait patiently for God's clearer direction. Submission calls for vulnerability—to place our gifts and expectations selflessly in the hands of another and together wait to see how they will be used by God.

> ## Lend an Ear
>
> *Scripture reminds us over and over that real love requires sacrifice. Loving spouses will put the other person first. This involves respect and support. Respect is giving your husband the freedom to grow spiritually and to grow in his career or other interests. Stephan does that for me as he encourages my gifts, talents, and friendships. A lack of respect devalues your spouse by not believing his feelings or interests are worthwhile.*
>
> *Support is an awareness of what your husband faces day in and day out, and trying to be empathetic and caring. We need to show an appreciation for our spouse and take time to listen—to what's on his mind.*
>
> *—Gigi*

The other day a woman said to me, "Well, I need to go get my degree to be fulfilled. So I'm going to leave my three children who are in elementary and high school and go 250 miles to college." It's hard for me to believe that is God speaking. When God does something, he doesn't just work on one objective (in this case education). Rather, he works on every relationship in our lives, bringing them to a discernible plateau or change that releases something else in our life. And in God's timing, all that he has gifted us to do will be completed.

I feel if we're really trying to do the will of God in our lives, and be under mission to each other, then he will tell us where he wants us to be. It may not be audible voices from Sinai, but there will be times when we feel—and our husbands will feel—it's time to move. Sometimes we may feel like we're being shoved, as was the case when I became part of the Trio. But everything in our lives will confirm a right decision with a quiet peace—even in the storms around us.

Fanning the Flame in a Marriage

It's important to Johnny that the our front steps be swept clean. But since the inside of the house is more important to me, I often forget to sweep the steps. He knows this, so when I do try to remember to sweep the walk, he appreciates it. Setting aside our own desires to serve our husband will fan the flame in a marriage. It's helpful to ask the question, "What could I do this day to serve my husband?"

—Susan

That was certainly the case with my recent decision to finish up work on my master's degree. I had been taking graduate courses in dribs and drabs—with Bill's blessing—for several years. Then my professor told me I would start loosing credits if I didn't finish my master's work.

So I got serious about it. With two daughters married and my son, Benjy, in college himself, I felt God's gentle release for me to pursue this direction. And by being able to schedule classes on Monday and Wednesday, I was able to keep weekends free for major concert dates.

Also affirming of my decision was the opportunity graduate school afforded me to build an even deeper relational bond with my oldest daughter, Suzanne. She was also working on her master's in literature, so we took many of the classes together. We discussed all the books together, shared with each other papers we were writing. We even competed for grades!

Class night became *our* night. We had dinner together, then spent three hours in class together, then drove home together. It became a special time just for the two of us—a time of God's own making.

I truly believe that God coordinates everything in our lives. The catch is that we don't always allow him the opportunity. Without being "under mission to" someone who is, himself, under mission to you, you stand to miss out on the possibilities and promises that God intends for your life.

Had I had my way, perhaps I would have been teaching literature at some national or internationally-known university. But God had other ideas; and thanks to my "husband under mission" to me, I was let in on the plan.

To His glory.

Gloria's Prayer
Gloria Gaither

Lord, let me hear your call to be "under mission to" persons in my life: my spouse, my children, my parents, my employees, my associates. And may I be the bridge of servanthood between them, giving them the courage to serve each other by creating an atmosphere of "preferring one another" myself.

Help me submit to those who might consider me an authority over them as you did when you chose to wash the feet of the weakest disciple. Let me be at ease and comfortable with the words: "You are right," "Please forgive me," "I'm sorry," or "That's a better idea."

Let me be so aware of your love and acceptance of me that I can say these words freely both to those in authority over me and to those who are under my authority.

Lord, let love be the tool I use today to rake level the ground around me, as your sacrifice of love made level the ground at the foot of the cross.

Make It Happen

1. Come right out and ask your husband what encourages him. Ask for specific examples, such as "What enables you to overcome setbacks?" or, "Who is the most encouraging person you have ever known and how did he encourage you?"

2. Think about a quality you'd like to change in yourself. Then ask for your husband's help in making that change. Go so far as to tell him *how* he can best help you.

3. Write out your personal version of a submission prayer, similar to Gloria's but using your own words to make submission something real in your marriage.

Chapter 13

HOW CAN WE GROW SPIRITUALLY AS A COUPLE?
Susan Alexander Yates

hen Johnny and I speak at conferences, one common concern I frequently hear women voice is that as a couple they seem to be on opposite spiritual tracks. While the wives seem to be digging deeper into the Word, the husbands are content with only attending Sunday worship services. I've even been asked, by women burdened with guilt, "Should I be doing something so we don't grow apart spiritually?"

When it comes right down to it, spiritual growth is an individual responsibility. My personal walk with the Lord needs to be my first priority. If I'm walking with Christ and growing in him, I'll be able to bring more to the couple relationship. But I'm not responsible for my husband's spiritual relationship, and he's not responsible for mine.

On the other hand, we *can* encourage each other spiritually. And one of the most important tools we have available to us is prayer—for one another and with each other. Early in our marriage, a friend suggested two ways to pray for my husband: pray for schedules and relationships. So I've found it helpful to pray for specific things for my husband each day. One day I pray for his relationships with his staff—sensitivity to their needs or decisiveness in giving direction. Another day I pray for his relationships with our children, and so on. And each day I try to thank God specifically for one character trait he has given my husband.

Before your husband leaves for work, ask him, "What do you have to get done today?" or "Who will you be seeing?"

He might have a meeting with an employee or employer. He might be concerned about a business transaction. He could have a conflict with the man he works next to on the assembly line. By praying for him, you're saying without preaching that you value the spiritual dimension in your relationship.

Then, when he comes home, ask him about the request he shared: "How did it go with your boss?"

—❦—

It is important to pray *for* one another, but it is also a blessing to pray *together*. If you don't currently pray with your spouse, seriously consider making this a priority in your relationship. It may seem awkward at first, but Johnny and I have found the benefits to be so great.

Fortunately, even before we were engaged, we made it a point to pray with each other. We brought that discipline into our marriage, and we committed ourselves to never going to bed at night without praying together. It's never been a long prayer, usually it's just Johnny praying for the two of us. But it gives a benediction to the day, a blessing on our relationship.

Another thing praying together does is force us to face conflicts. It's really hard to pray with—and for—someone you're angry with. We have to get things straight between us before we pray. It doesn't mean we solve big problems right then; we just clear the air and offer forgiveness.

If you're just starting to pray together as a couple, remember it will take commitment. One couple in our church, who had been married a number of years, decided to start praying together. "But it feels so awkward," one of them finally admitted. We assured them that's normal. Any new dimension in a relationship is awkward. We then suggested the following simple approach.

First, you share one need or concern and have your husband pray for you. Then your husband will share one concern and you will pray. Finally, in unison, pray the Lord's Prayer. Most church-goers feel comfortable reciting that prayer with somebody. Over time, praying for each other will become a comfortable, sweet experience.

You can also encourage your husband's spiritual growth by sharing what you have learned about God on your own. Tell him what you read in the Bible, what you heard on the radio or at a conference.

A friend of mine once said, "Interpretation without application is abortion of Scripture." I thought that was a radical statement, but he had a point: If we don't apply God's Word to our lives, we won't remember it.

Don't Quench the Fire

While most women would say they want to encourage their husband's spiritual growth, sometimes our actions deny it. Some friends of mine were looking for a church, and I encouraged the wife to go ahead and attend a church her husband liked since she was getting plenty of spiritual support and nourishment from Bible Study Fellowship. It turned out he loved the church—he's there every time the door is open. And he's growing spiritually. When we see that our husband is starting to spark a little bit, we need to be so careful not to discourage it.

—Gigi

Consequently, when Johnny and I share a verse with each other, we try to think, "How can we apply this?" Or when we run into a difficult situation, we ask, "What spiritual promise would apply in this situation?"

There are times I'm tempted to complain about my husband. When I feel a complaint session coming on, I stop for a moment and recite Philippians 4:8 to myself: "Finally, brothers, whatever is true, whatever is noble, whatever is right, whatever is pure, whatever is lovely, whatever is admirable—if anything is excellent or praiseworthy—think about such things." Then I ask myself, *How does that apply to my attitude toward Johnny?* It's important that we not fall into a habit of negative thinking.

Often women are more in tune with their spiritual needs or more vocal about their spiritual concerns and triumphs. For that reason, it's possible, as you share with your husband, to communicate that you're a "better" Christian than he is. Remember, we don't all grow at the same rate or in the same way. You might go through a time when you've plateaued spiritually and your husband may step in and encourage you. We need to grant one another grace in those situations and allow growth to happen at its own rate.

God speaks to each of us in different ways. The expression of our faith may be different, our spiritual gifts may be different. God is not going to make us copies of one another.

I have a married friend who feels called to a life of contemplation. She spends a great deal of time in solitude and prayer. She's pulling back from a lot of involvement and leadership. That's a unique calling God has given her. I have another friend who is moving more and more into up-front leadership and discipleship. Neither one of these friends has a deeper walk than the other, they're merely different.

Spiritual growth is not a race. We're not competing. Spiritual growth is more like a walk through a garden. We're not sprinting to the finish line; we're walking from one incredible array of beauty to the next. Granted, there are weeds and rocks along the way, but we're exploring, not racing. We're both going to notice different things, and go through different seasons in our growth. And as we walk through that garden, we need to love one another, pray for one another, and learn from one another.

Men Have Needs, Too

I don't know any place in Christendom where there isn't a need for men discipling men. All too often men's fellowship groups have breakfast and watch football movies instead of really confessing and meeting each other's needs. Entertainment alone cannot supply what men are really hungering for—spiritual growth and support. Maybe being transparent with one another is embarrassing. Maybe our culture has convinced men they must be macho. But the truth is, all human beings—including men—really need support, nurture, and a place to be honest.

We could help our husbands by starting a couples' Bible study. Getting them involved with couples could pave the way for a group just for men.

—Gloria

For Johnny and me, spiritual growth is encouraged when we get away for a couple of days each August—just before the pressures of a new school year are upon us. During those few days we *very* informally examine ourselves and our children in five areas of growth: spiritual, physical, intellectual, emotional, and social. Many times we hit this retreat dog tired; and we'd just as soon vegetate than talk. But happily, conviction wins out over feelings and we eventually think through our needs in these five areas and establish goals for the coming year. In turn, these needs and goals become the foundation of our prayer petitions for the next twelve months. That's especially encouraging for me because I know Johnny is praying for each child in the same way I am. I feel real support.

This exercise is also great for couples who don't have children. It generates some great communication as you question and explore your needs.

"Is there a need for one special friend? Are you feeling lonely?" "Are you eating too much junk food? Do you need to get exercise? Do we need to alter our eating habits?" (For Johnny there is always the need for regular exercise. With all he needs to do, it's difficult to find time to fit in physical fitness.)

"Do you feel the need to be in a Bible study this year that you're not leading, where you can be fed, or do you feel the need to be discipling somebody? Memorizing Scripture?" A spiritual need for me might be a vision and plan for my quiet time. Maybe I've gotten lax and I need regular time with God to be my priority. This kind of communication gives us a way to be united in vision and be supportive in prayer.

Group retreats can also give your spiritual life a boost. If you feel like you're in a period of complacency or you're not growing, listening to some good teaching can revive you. You may receive excellent instruction in your home church, but it's refreshing to hear someone different on occasion.

If your church doesn't provide a retreat, there are many organizations that do. Many seminaries have short-term courses for a week or a weekend. It could be something specifically designed for couples, but it doesn't have to be. Attend something that will challenge you to grow in the Lord and grow in your marriage.

After you attend a retreat together, take time before you go home to talk about how the new insights you've heard will affect your life. This kind of conversation will help you make the most of the retreat experience.

A Word about Friends . . . Again

In a previous chapter, I mentioned the important role friends play in strengthening the marital bond. Well, friends can strengthen spiritual bonds as well. As you encourage your husband's spiritual growth, pray for other people to become involved in the process. We desperately need people to whom we're accountable. Women generally recognize this need before men. Consequently, wives need to encourage their husbands to have one or two friends with whom they get together with on a regular basis. They need other men who are believers, who will share with them, encourage, and pray for them.

Johnny has a friend named Charlie with whom he gets together every week at a local restaurant. They share their schedules, what they need prayer for, and how they're doing in their marriages.

This relationship gives Johnny a confidant. Often a man may have a concern he doesn't want to share with his wife because she has too much on her plate already, or he feels a man will understand better. Once a concern is shared, Charlie will hold Johnny accountable. Charlie can also offer advice and counsel as well as prayer support.

Anything you can do to encourage your husband to be involved with other believing men is important. At our church we have a men's night out. Usually there are about sixty men who come to hear a speaker and open up to each other. There are also men's retreats sponsored by other Christian groups in our area. Johnny went to one where there were about three hundred men who were vulnerable with each other and challenged to grow.

Not only is man-to-man encouragement valuable, but couple-to-couple encouragement is critical as well. Every Washington's birthday weekend, we get together with two other couples to review the highs and lows of the preceding year. We have a time of sharing, with one person at a time on "center stage."

On one occasion I shared my frustration over letting my prayer life with Johnny slide. The group's response was twofold. They *identified* with my frustration. They too were not satisied with their prayer lives as couples. I wasn't alone. And they *encouraged* me by committing themselves to pray specifically for Johnny and me in this matter.

This level of spiritual intimacy will not happen overnight. But the pursuit of such friendships is well worth the time and effort. The identification, encouragement, *and* accountability offered by a group of friends frees you and your husband from trying to be all things to each other. Moreover, these "benefits" can wonderfully work together in helping you and your husband grow into the kinds of people God wants you to be.

Another way to grow spiritually as a couple is to embark on a new project or ministry that forces us to step out of our comfort zone and help other people. Maybe it's adopting a single parent family. Perhaps it's spending a week's vacation going on a missions trip.

A friend of mine and her husband went with their church's youth group to volunteer at a community center in Chicago. She said, "The couple that ran the center was so on fire for the Lord that Ben and I were challenged to consider the depth of our relationships with Christ. And we spent only a few hours with them." This kind of association with other believers can go a long way in nurturing growth in you and your husband.

Women need to leave their husband's spirituality up to the Lord. And that means we need to allow God the privilege of developing another person differently from the way he's developing us. But as you face the challenge of spiritual growth in marriage, remember God is *for you* and for your marriage. See those words as a declaration hanging over your bed—"God is for this marriage." Sometimes we forget that.

God desires your fellowship and knows you will be happiest when you are close to him. And as we encourage each other in our spiritual relationship, we will grow to echo the words of Asaph in Psalm 73:28: "But as for me, it is good to be near God."

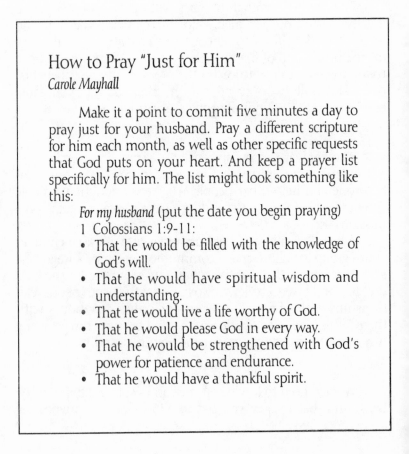

How to Pray "Just for Him"
Carole Mayhall

Make it a point to commit five minutes a day to pray just for your husband. Pray a different scripture for him each month, as well as other specific requests that God puts on your heart. And keep a prayer list specifically for him. The list might look something like this:

For my husband (put the date you begin praying)
1 Colossians 1:9-11:
• That he would be filled with the knowledge of God's will.
• That he would have spiritual wisdom and understanding.
• That he would live a life worthy of God.
• That he would please God in every way.
• That he would be strengthened with God's power for patience and endurance.
• That he would have a thankful spirit.

2. That he would develop a friendship with a committed Christian who would challenge him.

3. That God would give him a hunger and thirst for himself and his Word.

Write down the answers when they come and date them.

After a friend of mine had been praying specifically for her husband for several months, she called me, excitement lilting in her voice.

"Guess what!" she exclaimed. "Bill just told me a new co-worker asked him if he'd be willing to attend a new early morning Bible study, and Bill said *yes!* And something else. I tried not to show my astonishment when Bill brought home a brochure on a Marriage Enrichment weekend and said he'd signed us up to go."

My friend and I rejoiced together in this new beginning.

From Today's Christian Woman
(May/June 1991)

Make It Happen

1. Put accountability to work at home. Ask your husband to help you reach your goals of regular prayer, Bible reading, or attendance at a Bible study. As you share your goals with him and ask him to hold you to them, it will open the door for him to share with you.

2. Read biographies of saints of the faith and see what encouraged their growth. Some ideas: *In the Shadow of the Almighty* by Elisabeth Elliot, *The Hiding Place* by Corrie ten Boom, *Billy Graham* by John Pollock, *Wilberforce* by John Pollock.

3. Offer to team teach a Sunday school class. Whether it's

for young children or adults, preparation and presentation time can bring you closer to each other and help you grow in your spiritual understanding.

4. If you sense an interest in your husband for getting a men's group started, tell him you'll do whatever you can to help. Offer to help with organization by making phone calls or preparing bulletin announcements. Also, be a sounding board for his ideas.

5. Above all, pray for your husband and for your marriage daily. Ask God to show you ways in which you can help to build a stronger marriage team.

Chapter 14

WHAT IF MY HUSBAND ISN'T A CHRISTIAN?

Susan Alexander Yates

have several friends who are married to non-Christians, and I know how difficult it is for them. There's Sunday morning church service where they are surrounded by "complete" families. There's the frustration of trying to raise a child to know the Lord in a home where double standards can exist. And there are the times of guilt and gnawing concern for a husband who is not a believer.

Yet, if you are married to an unbeliever, you can find strength from this simple yet profound fact: Jesus understands. And this understanding is clearly stated in Hebrews 4:15-16: "For we do not have a high priest who is unable to sympathize with our weaknesses, but we have one who has been tempted in every way, just as we are—yet was without sin. Let us then approach the throne of grace with confidence, so that we may receive mercy and find grace to help us in our time of need."

Jesus understands your situation. He understands your agony, your loneliness, and your pain. You can, in turn, offer your pain back to God as a sacrifice. When it comes to handling hardships, I particularly remember author Elisabeth Elliot's words. She once said that sometimes when we're in a difficult situation we feel we have nothing to offer to the Lord. She suggested that our sufferings can be an offering to God. If we lift up our sufferings as an offering it makes them seem more worthwhile.

Although it's hard to accept at times, you need to remember that you are *not* responsible for your husband's salvation. Not long ago a woman came up to me after I had finished talking at a retreat. She told me a little about her life, and before long she was in tears. She felt tremendous guilt that her husband hadn't come to Christ. I assured her she was not guilty because of what her husband did or did not believe. Her husband's faith was between him and God. I encouraged the woman to be concerned that *she* grew in Christ. The Holy Spirit is the one who convicts of sin—not wives.

In 1 Peter 3, we're told to influence our husband not with words, but with a pure and reverent life. That doesn't mean you can't tell him what Christ is doing in your life; however, it does warn against brow beating him. One friend I know said she simply shared with her husband that she was going to begin praying daily for increased patience with their children. Over time, her husband did notice a change in how his wife handled the kids. When the time was right, she told him she attributed the new level of patience to answered prayer.

Also, you need to see your husband as a tool in your life, given by God to make you more like Jesus Christ. For instance, I know one woman who readily admits that her situation has made her dig deeper into the Bible for answers and encouragement—something she might not have done so passionately if her husband was a believer.

Your husband is not your adversary; he is your partner—for life. Therefore, a good question to ask yourself is, "Am I allowing this difficulty to draw me closer to the Lord or am I becoming bitter?" Tell God your hurts and disappointments and ask him to draw you closer to himself. Read his Word, and listen to him, for he has something special to teach you.

Common Dilemmas, Difficult Challenges

One of the difficult challenges in being married to a non-Christian is the spiritual nurturing of your children. There has been so much written on the male being the spiritual leader in the home that there can be a tendency for wives to become bitter if their husbands don't assume that role. However, since you're the one who knows Christ, God has called you to be the spiritual leader for this time. You must disciple your children.

> ## What Are You Feeling?
>
> *For some reason, many men are more intimidated spiritually than women. Maybe it's because they don't like to share their emotions as much as women do, and are not as relational as women. If we could encourage men to open up those emotional flood gates, they would begin to change spiritually.*
>
> *—Gigi*

It's important to be sensitive to your husband's feelings, but do not avoid teaching your children about Christ and their need for him. Maybe you need to find time to do this when Dad's not there so he doesn't feel awkward or get angry. Discuss with your husband your desire to teach the children about Jesus. Tell him exactly what you want to teach them or why you want to take them to Sunday school. And find out what spiritual values he would like communicated to his children and include what doesn't contradict Scripture. (See "A House Divided," page 145.)

As they get older, your children will recognize that their father doesn't believe what they do. Don't be critical of him for that. Your children need to sense that you love and respect him even though you are in a different place spiritually. As they mature, the children can join you in praying that their father will accept Christ.

We need to raise our kids with the strong conviction that they're God's people. Despite the fact that you're married to an unbeliever, we need to teach our children to marry believers. This is so important. Before they begin to date they need to know that God's plan for them is to marry a fellow believer.

Another common dilemma is how involved you should be in church. The answer lies with your husband. Will he go to church? Is he so antagonistic that he doesn't want you to go? Does he allow you to go, but won't go himself? Your level of involvement should not exceed his level of tolerance.

If your husband resents the time you spend at church, ask yourself, "Is there somewhere I can cut back? Or at least cut back on activities that conflict with our time together?" I'd cut out evening meetings, for example, and go to a daytime Bible study. It might be more important on Sunday nights to sit and watch a football game with him than to head back to church.

Don't Major on Minors

The biblical advice for influencing an unbelieving spouse is to be the kind of person who will make him not resent the Lord. It's important that we wives not major on "churchianity," but major on the things that Jesus taught—attitudes, reactions. Let's major on the fruits of the Spirit—patience, gentleness, kindness, long suffering, meekness; and spend a lot more time cultivating these things than talking to our husbands about religion. Often wives can win their husbands by being the kind of companion that by example says "You'd like Jesus if you got to know him."

—Gloria

Many women I know whose husbands are nonbelievers wish they could get their husband to church or a church-related event. However, I think it's important that we not try to manipulate anyone to Christ. There's a fine line between creating opportunities to hear the gospel and manipulation. If your husband feels like he's being ganged up on, you're pushing too hard.

A good place to start in encouraging your husband's involvement is with an activity that caters to his interests.

A friend of mine, whom I'll call Elsie, sings in our church choir. Her husband will come to church when she's doing a concert because he's interested in his wife's activities. He's also interested in people of other cultures. So when some Russian students spent two weeks with our church one summer, Elsie volunteered to house two of the Russian girls. That was a wonderful opportunity for Bob to be involved in the life of the church. And when we had a farewell at the church for the students, he was there because it was for "his" Russian kids. At the service, their leader was baptized, and Bob heard the gospel.

Kathy's husband is a real sports fanatic. The church's women's softball team needed a coach, so they asked Kathy's husband to coach them. The women took it upon themselves not to preach at him, but to make sure their attitudes reflected Christ. He coached them again the following summer and, in time, became a believer.

Bonnie's husband worked in concrete, and when the church needed some "extra hands" to work on a construction project, he agreed to help. Slowly, he became a regular church attender. So the principle is, watch for projects and programs your husband would enjoy being a part of—and then let him know about them.

Other people can also help. If your husband is social, have a dinner party and invite a few couples you think your husband would like. Once he has friends within the church, he'll feel more comfortable attending events.

If you think your husband would respond positively, ask a man from church to call him and invite him to a men's breakfast or father/son outing. He might feel less pressured if the invitation doesn't come from his wife.

Steps for Sustaining Your Own Spiritual Strength

One comment I've frequently heard from women married to unbelievers is that it's hard to come to church because it is so family-oriented. I really do wish more Christian couples would invite single people or those without their mates to sit with them during worship and include them in other church activities. This support and encouragement is vital since it enables women married to unbelievers to become part of the church family.

However, also important for "spiritual singles" is the opportunity to be in fellowship with others in similar circumstances. A woman in our church married before she was a believer. After she became a Christian, she started a group for wives of unbelievers called W.W.W.—Won Without a Word (based on 1 Peter 3:1). The group meets every other Thursday at noon so working women can attend. Their meetings aren't publicized. Instead, women find out about the group from other women or our church staff.

Minimize the Differences

The woman married to an unbeliever needs to be sensitive to all the things that she can do in her husband's world. Go to a ball game with him or go fishing. Keep the lines of communication open, supporting all the things that are not detrimental to your faith or relationship. By maximizing the things you can do together, it minimizes the differences, and strengthens your marriage.

—Gloria

Their purpose is to encourage one another to trust Christ, not commiserate together. They study books such as *Caught in the Middle* by Beverly Bush Smith and Patricia DeVorss (Tyndale), and Larry Crabb's *The Marriage Builder* (Zondervan). They discuss one chapter at each meeting and pray together.

I would also encourage a woman whose husband is not a believer to find a prayer partner. You can call one another when you are having a bad day or a good day. "Pray for me today because I'm struggling," or "Here's a blessing I've discovered."

It also helps to reach out to other people. My friend Elsie had an argument with her husband over a spiritual issue some time ago and she woke up the next morning feeling blue. Her thought was, *Well, I can either feel sorry for myself or I can reach out and care for somebody else.*

After breakfast, she got in her car and drove to a nearby nursing home. She spent the day visiting residents—talking, laughing, and encouraging them. By the time she left she was refreshed and encouraged herself because she reached out and cared for someone else. "If I hadn't been a person in pain, I'm not sure I would have done that," said Elsie. "When I care for others, I'm less likely to feel sorry for myself or discouraged since my husband doesn't share my passion for the Lord."

If your husband is not a believer, remember that many of the basics of a strong, happy marriage are not necessarily related to religious conviction. Good communication is still something you need to work on, as well as appreciating your husband, and admiring his positive traits. And you need to respect your husband. Ask for his opinion. Encourage him. Compliment him.

Consider developing common interests. Every couple needs to do that, but especially when spiritual values differ. This prevents spiritual differences from driving wedges between you. If he likes to sail, learn to sail. If he enjoys puttering around the garden, learn how to garden.

Finally, you can strengthen your relationship by praying for him. If he's comfortable with prayer, ask, "Honey, what concerns do you have that I can pray for today?" Many husbands will respond positively to being prayed for when it's done out of genuine concern, not an attempt to look pious. Answered prayer is a great way for an unbeliever to see the power of God. Such a testimony can become a vital step in bringing an unbelieving husband into the fellowship of faith.

A House Divided
Brenda Olcott-Reid

It isn't easy raising a child to be a Christian when your spouse is not. Studies have shown that most children whose parents are Christians become Christians themselves, while far fewer children with a Christian mom and non-Christian dad do so. But obstacles can be overcome, just as they were for Paul's helper Timothy. His mother was a Christian Jew; his father a non-believing Greek. Paul wrote to Timothy in 2 Timothy 1:5 and 3:14-15, "I have been reminded of your sincere faith, which first lived in your grandmother

Lois and in your mother Eunice and, I am persuaded, now lives in you also. . . . Continue in what you have learned and have become convinced of, because you know those from whom you learned it, and how from infancy you have known the holy Scriptures, which are able to make you wise for salvation through faith in Christ Jesus."

Here are some guidelines I've followed as I try to instill faith in my children despite my husband's unbelief.

Present Christ to your spouse gently. Bill and I discuss Christianity from time to time. When the opportunity allows, I present biblical precepts and ask him to consider them, but I don't urge him to make a decision for Christ. He would see it as nagging, and it would do more harm than good. First Peter 3:1-2 says, "Wives, in the same way be submissive to your husbands so that, if any of them do not believe the word, they may be won over without words by the behavior of their wives, when they see the purity and reverence of your lives." Just as with your children, our example matters much more to our spouse than our words.

Pray for your family daily. Being the spiritual head of a family by default is quite a responsibility, and sometimes it seems overwhelming. We need to pray for ourselves to set a good example, to be a good parent even if our spouse doesn't become a Christian soon, and for our children to follow Christ despite the circumstances. We also need to ask for forgiveness for our mistakes and lapses, and press on to greater spiritual maturity.

Attend worship services and Sunday school with your spouse's blessing. Most non-Christians don't mind if their spouse and children go to church once a week, or more frequently if it's during Lent or Advent. But a non-believer can feel deserted if you attend church all day Sunday as well as mid-week services and evening church meetings. He may also feel that the kids are getting "too much religion" if it seems they're always off at youth group meetings and outings. Respect your spouse's feelings, and limit your church commitments to those that won't detract from your family life.

Resist attempts from others at church to make you feel guilty about not attending as often as other families. When an entire family is Christian, church activities can bring them together, but when one parent is a non-Christian, the same activities can be divisive.

Sing Christian songs. While pushing the girls on the swings or taking a walk in the woods, I sing songs about Jesus and God's world. They especially love our expanded version of "Oh, How I Love Jesus," as we go through all our relatives and friends singing, "Yes, Jesus loves Karen; yes, Jesus loves Papa; yes, Jesus loves Travis; 'cause Jesus loves everyone."

Point out God's workings and thank him frequently. We have many natural opportunities to express thanks to God for his beautiful world and all his care: while picking fruit, while driving past a field of wheat, while watching the clouds or rain or sunset or stars, while splashing in the wading pool or building a snowman, or when we see the first spring flower bloom or the trees change color each fall. I want my children to see God in all aspects of life, and so far they have.

Stimulate your family to ask questions about God, heaven, and the Bible. Since Cathy was three she's asked questions about what happens when people die and what heaven is like. Answer all questions truthfully, to the extent your child and non-believing spouse can understand. Look up answers in the Bible, or help your older children look them up.

With older children and teens, honest family discussions about each member's beliefs can clear up misconceptions and help everyone better understand each other. Don't shy away from such discussions for fear that your spouse's lack of belief will erode your children's faith. Our children are sure to discuss the "big questions" of life and death with non-believing friends at school or college. If your child hears a Christian response to agnosticism or atheism, he might be better prepared to respond at a later date.

Encourage and praise your children's effort at helping and sharing. Toddlers love to "help," and if they are allowed to participate when possible and praised for their efforts, even when the results aren't the best, they'll grow up with a love for serving others. Sharing comes less naturally, but when children are praised for sharing, they'll grow up wanting to share. Encourage your children to share time and things with those in need. With your spouse's consent, let them participate in whatever offerings you make to the church or to charity.

If, like me, you never seem to have enough time and your spouse, like mine, balks at giving too much money, just remember the widow's mite and the little boy's five loaves and two fishes. Jesus is pleased when you and your children give whatever time and money you can.

Balance secular and Christian themes in holidays. Your appeals to limit the involvement of Santa Claus or the Easter Bunny in your holiday celebrations need to be weighed against your spouse's desire to continue family traditions.

Bill and I compromise on this. We read stories

about Santa and his reindeer but we've told the girls from the beginning that these are just make-believe stories, while the story of Jesus' birth actually happened. Bill goes along with lighting candles on an Advent wreath, reading Bible passages, and singing hymns during the four Sundays before Christmas. The girls help us place the presents under the tree so they know where they come from, and we try to limit the number of presents. On Christmas morning, before we open any presents, we light candles on birthday muffins and sing happy birthday to Jesus. They also help set up a manger scene that Bill bought as a present for me one Christmas.

Do your best, with God's help, and leave the results to God. "There is no fear in love," says 1 John 4:18. As each child and your spouse follow their own trail in life, entrust them to God. When they reach a crossroad, pray for them and point them to God's guidance, but realize they must each choose their own path. See your children as individuals, not as extensions of you. In doing so, you won't feel overly responsible for their choices, and later successes and failures. In the words of Ruth Graham, "In raising children, all you can do is your best. If your child ultimately grows up to honor God, consider it a miracle. We can do the possible but we can't do miracles. So we take care of the possible and leave the impossible to God."

From Today's Christian Woman
(January/February 1991)

Make It Happen

1. If there is not currently a support group for wives of unbelievers in your church, talk to your church leaders about starting one. Be willing to take on much of the work yourself, even if you aren't the group's leader. There will be lots of phone calling, research, and other preparation to be done. To start with, set up prayer partners. This may naturally grow into a support group.

2. On days you're struggling, find a way to minister to others. Follow the example of Elsie in this chapter and visit a nursing home. Or spend some time with a lonely neighbor. Do something to get your focus off yourself and onto others.

3. Develop a specific plan for your children's religious upbringing. Don't share the entire plan with your husband—that would overwhelm him. Fill him in as you go along. Show him the books you're going to read to your young children. When they're old enough for children's clubs at church, describe the club to your husband and see if he would object. Discuss each stage of this education with your husband so he knows you respect him and your marriage.

4. If there isn't a good avenue for your husband to participate in your church activities, talk to the church leaders about starting something that could include nonbelieving men. Possibilities include sports teams, men's breakfasts, camp outs, construction projects, or father/child activities.

TRUTHS WORTH REMEMBERING

s they answered the questions presented in this book, Gloria, Gigi, and Susan consistently referred to four "truths" as being absolutely essential to any and every marriage.

The first truth concerns *the importance of good verbal communication*. The need for talk time is classic marriage advice. And for good reason. Problems are rarely solved without discussion. If you can't talk about it, you can't resolve it.

Another recurring truth that often falls victim to our hectic schedules and misplaced priorities is *the need to spend time together as husband and wife*. Overcoming a feeling of loneliness, nurturing spiritual growth—so many of the concerns women express can be confronted by spending time with their spouse. Work toward establishing weekly or biweekly date nights. Spend time doing all those things you used to do—and enjoy—before life became too busy.

A third essential truth is *the need for commitment*. Some of the problems in your marriage will seem insurmountable. But if your underlying assumption is "we're in this for the long haul," you're more likely to overcome your obstacles than to become buried beneath them.

The fourth and final truth is foundational to all of the above. Indeed, it is foundational to any marriage that calls itself Christian. That truth is *the absolute necessity to put God first*. It is God alone who enables us to forgive our husbands, to lovingly encourage them, or to offer the kind of support they need. Consequently, our marriages will grow as our walk with the Lord grows.

We trust you were challenged by these and other "truths" presented throughout this book: Great truths that will help you have a great marriage.

Today's Christian Woman is a positive, practical magazine designed for contemporary Christian women of all ages, single or married, who seek to live out biblical values in their homes, workplaces, and communities. With honesty and warmth, *Today's Christian Woman* provides depth, balance, and perspective to the issues that confront women today.

If you would like a subscription to *Today's Christian Woman* send your name and address to *Today's Christian Woman*, P.O. Box 11618, Des Moines, Iowa 50340. Subscription rates: one year (6 issues) $14.95, or two years (12 issues) $23.60.